James Barr
Princeton
February 1962.

LAW AND GRACE

by the same author

A CHRISTIAN THEOLOGY
OF THE OLD TESTAMENT

and in the Torch Bible Commentaries

ESTHER, SONG OF SONGS, LAMENTATIONS
RUTH AND JONAH
HOSEA

LAW AND GRACE

Must a Christian Keep the
Law of Moses?

GEORGE A. F. KNIGHT
Professor of Old Testament History and Theology,
McCormick Theological Seminary, Chicago

SCM PRESS LTD
BLOOMSBURY STREET LONDON

© GEORGE A. F. KNIGHT 1962
FIRST PUBLISHED 1962
PRINTED IN GREAT BRITAIN BY
BILLING AND SONS LTD
GUILDFORD AND LONDON

CONTENTS

CONTENTS

INTRODUCTION

IT is a fact of our time that more and more people are becoming aware of the significance of the Old Testament for the Christian faith. It may be that these very people were brought up to consider that the New Testament alone is the source of Christianity. If so, they may have been in the habit of using expressions like: 'The New Testament basis of our faith . . .,' 'The Church of the New Testament . . .,' and so on. The Bible as a whole is a bulky book. In consequence the people of whom we are thinking perhaps possess and use for all practical purposes a pocket size New Testament, to which, as a great concession, may be attached at the back the book of Psalms out of the Old Testament. They thereby tacitly accept the principle that this neat little 'book' of theirs contains the whole source of the Church's faith.

That attitude to the Bible, as I say, is passing. The whole Bible is indeed bulky, and therefore difficult to handle. But then the life that we must live today is also more complex than men imagined it to be in days of old. This generation of churchmen is coming to realize that the Old Testament must be taken quite as seriously as the Church has been in the habit of taking the New Testament. The Old Testament has much to say about great areas of life that the New Testament does not touch on. Historically, the Church has always declared that the Bible comprises the two Testaments. It has recognized that, before the New Testament was written, the Old Testament was in fact *the* Scriptures of the Church. The New Testament itself actually speaks of the Old Testament as 'the Scriptures'. In its liturgical practice the Church has always used the Old Testament along with the New, and read the first lesson from it. But we are only now giving the Old Testament the rightful place it should enjoy in our private reading of the Bible and in our theological enquiries.

We are being forced to do so, moreover, by the very nature of the problems that the Church is facing in our generation. Many countries have emerged from the Second World War as welfare states; that is to say, political units in which the citizens have been forced to discover anew their essential brotherhood. We live in a world where Communism is a hard fact to be reckoned with, again a form of social development where the community is to the fore. Our own society today is actually much less individualistic than it has ever been in history. Great numbers of men and women now take their ideas from the mass media of communication that we have developed, such as the Sunday newspapers and television. Again, within the factory the individual may scarcely dare think for himself; outside it, he has lost the desire to do so. The challenge that the New Testament Gospel makes to the individual soul and conscience as it seeks to create a new community is therefore very hard for the individual to understand and still harder for him to face. Yet it is of course the *Old* Testament that deals in the first place with man as a group, man-in-a-nation, man as community man, and only secondly with individual men as members of a human society.

In the Old Testament, moreover, the purpose and plan of God for the world are proclaimed, not primarily to individuals, but first to whole groups or communities or nations. No wonder then that we are recognizing today the need to restudy the Old Testament. We have rediscovered in our time that the New Testament does not contain the whole of the Christian Gospel; if it did contain it all, then the Church would have discarded the Old Testament long ago. On the other hand, many of the great insights of the Old Testament and the great basic truths which it contains are actually needed as never before in the situation that atomic age man finds himself in. We are therefore now seeing ever more clearly because of our new situation that the two elements that comprise the textbook of the Christian faith must be reunited in the thinking of us all if we are to possess a 'whole' Gospel capable of meeting the needs of modern industrial man. In other words, we must once again integrate 'the Law' with 'the Gospel', a thing which the Church did actually succeed in doing at a number of periods in the more distant past, but which it has been failing to do since the Victorian era.

Such a statement presents us at once, of course, with the need to clarify our terms. For example, we may ask, what do we mean by the word 'Gospel', and more particularly, what do we mean by the word 'Law'? 'The Law was given by Moses,' declares John 1.17, 'but grace and truth came by Jesus Christ.' Does such a statement imply that Jesus Christ has superseded the Law? Does it mean that 'grace' and 'truth' are ideas first made known only in Christ, and that consequently they did not exist in Old Testament times? If so, then how are we to explain the fact that the words 'grace' and 'truth' are both Old Testament words? Then this word 'Law'. What exactly does it mean? Is it that which Moses mediated at Mount Sinai? Is it the Ten Commandments? Or even is it synonymous with the Old Testament understanding of God's revelation as a whole? What did Paul mean when he pitted the Law, as it might seem, against the Gospel which had come to earth in Christ? If the Old Testament is still accepted by the Church as part of Christian Scripture, can we then say that any of it is of consequence no longer? If Leviticus and Numbers have been fulfilled in Christ, then why do we need to bother about reading them now? And have they any possible word to say to the modern Christian in a western democratic state?

These then are just some of the questions we shall have to try to answer if we are to understand the present-day trend which is to integrate 'Law' and 'Gospel', and see why re-habilitating the Old Testament in the eyes of today's generation is such a marked feature of present-day theology.[1] For although, as we have said, the Church itself recognizes clearly that the first part of the book of God's Revelation to his Church and world, the Old Testament, is nothing less than sacred Scripture, yet many individuals within the Church have still far to go before they are in the position to appreciate the significance of what the Church is trying to say.

[1] See, e.g., T. W. Manson, *Ethics and the Gospel*, 1960.

I

The Gospel

IT would seem to be superfluous to declare what the Gospel is. We shall therefore not seek to do so at this point. We shall begin by observing what meaning and content various persons or groups find in it.

It is easy for us to see certain aspects of the Gospel so clearly that we emphasize them to the exclusion of all else. We may see, and in so seeing, be making a valid judgment, that the Gospel gives individual souls a sense of peace and power such as the world knows nothing of. This is true; the Gospel does just that. We may see that the Gospel may accomplish what no psychiatrist can effect. It can wholly transform a man's life and outlook because by believing it he finds that his guilt has been met and his sordid past has been totally forgiven. This also is true. We may see the Gospel healing the bodies of men and through faith men throwing away their crutches and walking. The Gospel does this too. We may see the Gospel as the God-given means whereby men learn to live together as brethren, as the means of reconciliation between employer and employee, between black and white, between East and West. The Gospel is just this bridge. We may see the Gospel to be the summons to young men and women to present their bodies as a living sacrifice, and give themselves unsparingly to lead a youth club, teach in a school in Africa, or nurse in a mental hospital. The Gospel does have this power. Or we may see the Gospel as the impelling motive towards prison reform, towards nuclear disarmament, towards the rehousing of the people, towards the socialization of the land or of the means of production. Many have found it to be so. Or again, we may see the Gospel as the means to bring a parish community together in fellowship in the parish church, there to worship God in piety and hope, and so to enter into the great heritage of worship their fathers knew. No one will doubt that the Gospel has done this more frequently than anything else.

Yet the Gospel means still other things as well. Other people see it as the justification of their very sincerely held hopes and plans for the good of all mankind. Some see it as the basis of all true civilization. Others see it as the only hope for mankind for the future. Others again see it as a message to be proclaimed to individual sinners, in the hope that they will be born again according to a pattern that many would declare is the one and only true and valid pattern, if a man is ever to enter into the Kingdom of God. In fact, 'the Gospel' means many things to many men.

Now, we ought to face the fact, if Christian humility is to be part of our Christian approach to our brethren, that these many understandings of what the Gospel is may each and all be, so far as they go, true and valid. There are men and women around us, sincere we believe them to be, but misguided we are sure they are, who declare categorically that 'the Gospel means the abolition of *Apartheid*', and they can see nothing else but that; or who are sure that 'the Gospel means the saving of the individual's soul', or 'the Gospel means the possibility of healing by faith all the sicknesses of men'. Yet, even while we ruminate on the fact that they have grasped only a part of the whole Gospel, we on our part are tacitly revealing what we believe the Gospel to be by the way we speak. The onlooker, therefore, is in the position to see that our understanding of the Gospel may be, in fact, just as narrow as is theirs. The Gospel is so great, so comprehensive, so all-embracing, that it is beyond the mind of any one of us to know what it really is. Remembering the need for humility, we must never condemn another Christian for seeing the heart of the Gospel to be something different from what we suppose it to be. Rather we should praise God that the Gospel is the *whole* answer to every need of his very complex world. One man applies part of it here, another there. One denomination preaches one area of it here, another emphasizes another aspect of it there. No one individual, no one church, possesses the whole Gospel, far less preaches it as a whole. Twenty years ago the church of our own choice or birth preached it differently from the way it proclaims it now, and very differently from the way it was proclaimed before the Reformation . . . and so on.

We can then, each and all of us, find justification for the Gospel we believe in the pages of the New Testament. 'I am of Paul, I am of Apollos' (cf. I Cor. 1.12). Even within the Roman Catholic Church, which believes that it possesses the whole truth of Christ within itself, the same departmentalized view of the Faith obtains. We are astonished to read sermons preached in the fourteenth century. The Marian orders concern themselves with the centrality of the Blessed Virgin Mary; the Dominicans with the study of the Word; the Franciscans with practical charity towards the underprivileged, and so on. Then where are we to find expressed that *wholeness* of the Christian Gospel which none of us as individuals or as churches can fully grasp? Is there some outside objective standard to which we may turn, that is not the Church itself, and is certainly not the conceptions of individual men within any one church, to which we may turn and look and say: '*That* is the Gospel for us all to proclaim'? Yes, of course there is. It is *the Gospel as it is*

*contained in the Old and New Testaments that together
comprise our Bible,* and the Church, both reformed and un-
reformed, has always said as much throughout the Christian centuries. This does not mean that the Bible contains
all that we can ever know of God. Our Lord himself promised us that the Holy Spirit in days to come would lead us
into greater truth. Yet any truth that the Church has
learned throughout the centuries has been based securely
upon the 'once-for-all' nature of the biblical revelation (see
p. 107).

It is obvious that a statement like the above needs clari-
fication for a generation that has been brought up to accept
as axiomatic that the Gospel is to be found in the New
Testament alone. Especially is this so when we see how the
wholeness of the Gospel has been mislaid in our generation,
and we each and all declare with conviction to be Gospel
what is in reality only part of that whole. If it is the case
that 'the Gospel' is in some sense contained in the Old
Testament as well as in the New Testament, then we are
forced back to the question with which we began when we
found ourselves faced with the seeming antithesis we have
already quoted from John's Gospel: 'The Law was given by
Moses, but grace and truth came by Jesus Christ.' Are we
not being forced to ask ourselves what this word 'Law' must
mean even before we seek to define the meaning of 'Gospel'?
For the idea of 'Law' is possibly already included in the
word 'Gospel' itself.

One of Germany's foremost preachers is Professor Helmut
Thielicke. In the ruins of the battered and bombed city of
Stuttgart he ministered to a needy people as they nightly
faced destruction and death. One would perhaps presuppose
that the Gospel alone could meet the needs of men and
women in such a plight. But 'Thielicke's preaching is
preaching of the Word of God, which is always both judg-

ment and grace, both Law and Gospel' declares his translator.[1] The relationship between Law and Gospel is evidently an important issue for those who would understand the relationship between the two Testaments.

[1] H. Thielicke, *The Waiting Father*, trans. J. W. Doberstein, 1960 (published in USA as *Our Heavenly Father*).

FOR FURTHER READING

James D. Smart, *The Interpretation of Scripture*, 1961.

A. G. Hebert, *The Authority of the Old Testament*, 1947.

Paul S. Minear, *Eyes of Faith*, 1948.

Alan Richardson, *Preface to Bible Study*, 1943.

James G. S. S. Thomson, *The Old Testament View of Revelation*, 1960.

H. H. Rowley, *The Faith of Israel*, 1956.

Alan Richardson, *An Introduction to the Theology of the New Testament*, 1958.

J. S. Whale, *Christian Doctrine*, 1942.

2

The Law

I'LL have the law on you,' declares the outraged housewife within a democratic state. She speaks as she does,
because she has been brought up to be aware of and to
trust in a justice that is imposed and regulated by the State
impartially on behalf of all citizens. She can therefore rely
upon this justice to prevent her neighbour from misusing
her freedom, and so from injuring her. She feels she can
turn to 'the man in blue' with complete conviction that she
will receive from the law which he represents an impartial
hearing. For she has been brought up to accept as basic to
her whole way of life that the 'law of the land' is her ally
and her friend, and the ground of her confidence for a true
relationship with her neighbours and society. But that is
not at all what the word 'law' meant for the writer of the
Fourth Gospel when he declared that the law was given by
Moses, though it is what it may mean for us.

John was writing in the days of the unquestionably
mighty Roman empire. To one born into the Roman empire in the first Christian century it was axiomatic to equate
the Roman empire with the civilized world as it was known.
Beyond the empire were strange and fierce tribes and cus-
toms, just as for us today on the planet Venus and Mars
there may live strange and inhuman creatures. This mighty
civilization and state of Rome was held together, let us
remember, not primarily by the dictatorship of a Caesar,
but by law, by that *lex* which the true Roman citizen

heartily revered. Caesars might come and Caesars might go, but consuls and proconsuls in the far corners of the empire continued to administer the *lex* of Rome upon which all else was built. And pagans and conquered tribes learned a new sense of security such as they had never known before when they put themselves under the justice of the *lex* of Rome. A man like St Paul could appeal to it in distant Palestine and be transported all the long way to Rome. This meant that he did not receive an arbitrary judgment on the spot given by an arbitrary judge. This was because the *lex* of Rome was something more profound and comprehensive than the whims of a mere Felix or a Festus. Roman law had been built up over the centuries even when the form of the Roman state vastly altered in the passage of time. Roman law continued to knit the vast and complex empire together as one, even when its far ends were quite out of touch with each other. Moreover, Roman law later continued to be the warp and woof of European life even when Rome itself fell before the onslaught of the barbarians who took control of the empire. Roman law moreover has developed into French law, Scottish law, American law, and has become the warp and woof of the justice upon which western man depends, so that the housewife of many lands today can exclaim with utter confidence 'I'll have the law on you . . .' Yet Roman *lex* is *not* what John was talking about when he spoke of the Law of Moses. It is necessary to be clear on this point, because many people immediately associate the biblical word 'law' with the heritage which the Roman empire left to posterity.

The Law of Moses must obviously then be something very different. We watch the Roman empire grow and develop in strength and might. Simultaneously it grows in thought and understanding, until it has produced some of the world's greatest men of action. These all took their stand upon the Roman *lex* that was the foundation of their life. But Roman law originally grew out of Roman religion. Religion and law, from time immemorial, have begun as twins in their early days. But Roman religion grew less and less meaningful as the years advanced. *Lex* itself grew out of the religious conception of *fas*. It was early believed that the founders of the Roman state had made a compact with certain deities. The latter guarded Rome; the Romans in turn had to fulfil certain clearly defined duties laid upon them. These were the *ius divinum* which Rome distinguished from the *ius humanum*. The latter covered human relationships apart from the gods altogether. By the time the New Testament was written, however, there was only one conception of law remaining in Rome, and in it the old gods no longer had any place.

Before the Christian era had begun, Roman religion had thus quite lost its hold upon educated men. It continued to be upheld by the state only in a stunted form, but now it had virtually no influence upon the life of the people. What really continued to have influence upon the empire was Roman *lex*, not Roman religion. We have not yet, of course, reached the point where we may profitably establish what the Law of Moses is, yet we know very well indeed that any parallel between Roman *lex* and the Mosaic Law is quite incomplete. We know that the Law of Moses was vitally concerned with *religion*, though the Roman law was not. John, then, was not seeing the Law of Moses in any sense in the light of Roman (or English!) law.

What then about the law as the Greeks knew it? After all, the New Testament was originally written in Greek, the Old Testament had been translated into Greek a couple of centuries before St Paul's day, and St Paul himself had chosen to expound the Gospel to the 'Greek' world by means of the Greek language.

In the Greek language the word *themis* is a word which
often translates our word 'law'. But once again *themis* does
not convey what we mean by our English word. *Themis* is
more nearly 'custom' than 'law'. It stands for what has
'always been done'; it is the 'done thing' now made statu-
tory. *Themis* is what a man has to learn today when he
joins a regiment or the staff of a public school in England
or a college in America. 'From time immemorial it has been
the custom here that at 6 p.m. on Fridays we . . .' A custom
such as is meant here is, however, still only an 'unwritten
law'. The Greeks wrote theirs down and even classified them.
The word they used for this written (though sometimes
also unwritten) code of what had always been the done thing
was *nomos*, and this is the word that the Fourth Gospel
uses in our quotation for 'law'. That then was how the
Greeks thought of law. But we can see at a glance once
again that it was certainly not what the Hebrews meant by
the word, or what John meant in his famous dictum.

The Hebrews were a Semitic people. Both their language
and their culture had developed from those current in the
'fertile crescent' that stretched from the borders of Egypt
northward and then east round the deserts of Arabia till
it became one with the great Mesopotamian plain. The
Sumerians, who preceded the Semitic peoples of the Tigris-
Euphrates valley, as well as the Aryan Hittites of Central
Anatolia, were both nations with highly developed codes of
law. Thus when the Semitic nations rose into ascendancy
during the third millennium BC in the Mesopotamian plain,
as so often happens, they took over much of the cuture of
those who had preceded them. The basis of Babylonian law
was therefore ready to hand. Nor was the great and justly
famous lawgiver King Hammurabi of Babylon (eighteenth
century BC) even the first of the important Near Eastern lawmakers. But the magnitude and importance of ancient

Babylonian law only became known to the modern world at the beginning of this century, when Hammurabi's 'code' of law was discovered, translated, and published in western languages. This code of law was found at Susa by a Frenchman called de Morgan and is now preserved in the Louvre. It is a rounded slab of black diorite stone on which King Hammurabi caused to be incised in the cuneiform writing of his day some 300 carefully tabulated laws. Biblical students noticed at once how similar some of its enactments were to others in the Mosaic Code. Read, for example, Ex. 21.28 and compare it with Hammurabi's code, clause 250: 'If a mad bull has rushed upon a man and gored him, so that he dies, that case has no remedy.' Or compare Ex. 21.23, the principle of the *lex talionis* (an eye for an eye) with clause 196-7: 'If a man has caused the loss of a freeman's eye, his own eye shall be destroyed.' 'If he has broken a freeman's limb, his own shall be broken.' And so on.

The 'Law of Moses' has thus many features in common with the earlier codes of the Fertile Crescent. But before we examine them we should first of all ask ourselves what we mean when we speak about 'the Law of Moses' at all.

Archaeology has given us more information about the life and civilizations of the Fertile Crescent and of Egypt than we would have dared to hope a hundred or even fifty years ago. But one thing it has not as yet been able to do is to give us evidence for the person of Moses from outside of the biblical record. This does not mean that we should doubt the historicity of Moses. Far from it. So dominant in the Old Testament is the tradition about Moses and the Exodus from Egypt that it is quite obvious that historical fact lies behind those traditions, even if they are told for us in the form of saga and perhaps even overlaid with elements of legend. If there had been no person called Moses, then, humanly speaking, the people of Israel would not have come into existence. If there had been no person of Moses, we should have had to invent one to comply with all the elements in Israel's faith that look back to him and to his activities. But as to when he actually lived, and under which Pharaoh he led his people out of Egypt, archaeology cannot help us in any detail. Suffice it to say that the consensus of scholarly opinion (though some good scholars do not agree with the hypothesis) is that Moses led the Exodus from Egypt somewhere about the year 1270 BC, so that the Pharaoh who pursued the Israelites through the 'Reed Sea', as it is called in the Hebrew, was Pharaoh Rameses II. Be that as it may, Moses had lived throughout his formative years under the law of Egypt, one that, in its turn, was greatly influenced by the various laws of the Fertile Crescent which now looked back for their source to the Law of Hammurabi, of which we have spoken, and which itself would already be some five hundred odd years old in Moses' day.

The tradition is that Moses gave his people the Law at Mount Sinai, soon after they had escaped from bondage in the land of Egypt. How much of the Law Moses himself gave to Israel, and in what form it was couched, we are not now in the position to say. But we are not surprised to find that both the form and the content of many enactments closely resemble those which trace their ancestry to Hammurabi's code.[1]

It would be wrong to approach the Law of Moses with the idea that, because it is in the Bible, everything that Moses

[1] Completer parallels between the 'Law of Moses' and Hammurabi's code than the few verses cited above may be found in an Appendix to Wade's *Old Testament History* or in W. W. Davies' study *The Codes of Hammurabi and Moses*. These books list some of those enactments that appear in common, so as to make Moses' dependence upon his own past quite clear. For an English translation of the main ancient codes, see G. A. Barton, *Archaeology and the Bible* (1937); J. M. Powis Smith, *The Origin and History of Hebrew Law* (1931); and J. B. Pritchard (ed.) *Ancient Near Eastern Texts* (1950).

enacted must be original. It would be a false kind of law he would have left us if this had indeed been the case. This is because the life lived by the ancient Hebrews was no different in essence from that of their neighbours. The Hebrews were parents like the Amorites or the Moabites, gave their daughters in marriage, possessed oxen and sheep, lusted and killed as other men did. The legislation which Moses gave his people began, at least, on the same level as that which was common to the life of the common civilization of his day throughout the whole Near East.

But, as we have said, how much of the Law we are to attribute to Moses himself and how much of it grew, as law always grows, is quite another question. In the first place, certain 'codes' of law in the Pentateuch (the general name for the first five books of the Old Testament) may in essence be even older than Moses himself. For example, we find legislation in the book of Exodus that is concerned with early ritual. In the form we have it, it has been adapted to suit the religious worship connected with the cult of Yahweh (or Jehovah) in the days before the monarchy began with Saul or David. Again, no one doubts that the custom of blood revenge, with laws to control it, is a survival from primitive times. Moses may well have taken over cultic laws from the Kenites, the tribe to which his father-in-law, Jethro, belonged, and then adapted them for Israel's use. On the other hand, the elemental basis of the Ten Commandments, with their wonderful *ethical* emphasis, may well have been the work of Moses himself, as God put it in his heart to say on the slopes of Sinai. Yet it is easy to see that the commandment which begins 'Thou shalt not make unto thee any graven image' has suffered expansion in the course of the centuries, as later generations sought to expound it. Its original Hebrew could have been as short and incisive as the two commands embodied each time in two Hebrew words, viz., 'Thou shalt not kill', and 'Thou shalt not commit adultery'. For short, pithy commands like these are very easily memorized, and quickly taught by parent to child as one generation succeeds the other.

But it has long been noticed that much of the 'Law of Moses' is legislation for periods in Israel's history that Moses knew nothing of. While any critical introduction to the Old Testament may be consulted on this matter, suffice it to say that we obviously possess within the Pentateuch legislative material (1) from about the period of the Judges, or 1100 BC, (2) other material from about the time of the great prophets in the seventh and sixth centuries BC, and (3) even more material compiled after the return of Israel from Exile. Yet all this material in the Pentateuch as we have it now is clearly known in New Testament times as 'the Law of Moses'. Legal precepts must be explained and developed to suit ever new situations—yet they still remain the same original precepts.

The earliest known law code of England was promulgated by King Alfred. It was quite a small collection of laws. But of course it grew as the centuries went by. Yet it still remained the Law of Alfred, although the latter would hardly have recognized it a century later if he had come back from the dead to see it.

One way in which a law-code can grow is by the accretion to itself of 'case-law'. A judge has to make a new decision. Supposing that there are in existence no decisions on which he can build made already by a predecessor in office, the situation he has to face is therefore wholly new. But the decision he comes to now is thereafter added to the law which he has inherited, and becomes part of it in turn. A good instance in the Bible is to be found in I Sam. 30.24-25. There we read: 'As his part is that goeth down to the battle, so shall his part be that tarrieth by the stuff: they shall part alike (i.e. share alike). And it was so from that day forward, that he made it a statute and an ordinance for Israel unto this day.' This decision by a man who later was to become the important figure of mighty King David was naturally regarded by Israel's historians as a development of the Law of Israel, or the 'Law of Moses'. That is why it was actually incorporated into it later on, as if it had always been there. We find it in Num. 31.27.

There are several Hebrew expressions for the various elements that comprise the Law. The 'statute', for example, was a 'fixed decree'. The above decision by David was called a statute. The verb from which the noun is derived means 'to chisel out'. We can see how originally, then, a statute was a law cut in stone, just like the *stele* of Hammurabi on which he sought to preserve his law for all centuries to come.

The 'judgment' was the 'case-law' to which we referred above. We should note again that David's statute above, his immutable decision, was also called a judgment. That is to say it was a judicial decision that was now added to the law book of Israel. That is how, as we have seen, it became an element in the material found in the book of Numbers. There are many such judgments in the Pentateuch. But what is unique about the Mosaic Law is that it contained also many 'words', an element not to be found in any modern, or western, law books. For example, what we today call the Ten Commandments were not known by that title in the Old Testament itself. Deut. 5.22 shows us that the Decalogue was regarded as having been spoken to Moses by the very mouth of God. And so the writer can say: 'These *words* the Lord spake unto all your assembly in the mount . . .'

This factor leads us now to another aspect of the Mosaic Law which we must take fully into account if we are to compare it in any way with the Gospel. Later generations of Old Testament writers and lawmakers were wholly convinced that Israel stood in a unique relationship to her God, Yahweh, and that that relationship was regulated in terms of what they called a Covenant. Ex. 19 shows us Moses climbing up the slopes of Mount Sinai to meet and talk with God, and reports to us God's command to Moses which he is to take back to the Israelites waiting below. God says: 'Thus shalt thou say to the house of Jacob, and tell the children of Israel; ye have seen what I did unto the Egyptians, and how I bare you on eagles' wings, and brought you unto myself. Now therefore, if ye will obey my voice indeed, and keep my covenant, then ye shall be a peculiar treasure unto me above all people; for all the earth is mine; and ye shall be unto me a kingdom of priests, and an holy nation. These are the words which thou shalt speak unto the children of Israel' (Ex. 19.3-6).

God begins by reminding Israel of his prevenient grace, that is to say, of how he acted in love towards Israel *first*, before Israel was even aware of his grace at all. Then God imposes his Covenant upon Israel, which Israel must obey and keep. On God's part, Israel will then be his *segullah*. We may explain this word as follows. In olden days a king was the ultimate owner of everything in the land he ruled. He owned every building, every farm, every coin. But that kind of 'owning' could give him little personal satisfaction. Consequently in his palace he kept a treasure chest of his 'very own', in which he delighted to store the precious stones and *objets d'art* which he loved to handle. This treasure-box was his *segullah*. In the same way, God, who had made the whole earth, and to whom all nations belonged, looked now upon Israel as his own peculiar treasure. But Israel was not chosen just to bask in the love of her God. Just as God himself is holy, so Israel was to be holy, that is, different from other peoples. And since this passage was composed some time after the great Isaiah had expounded the meaning of holiness, our author would include a moral content in the word that was not present in earlier days when 'holy' only meant 'taboo'. As Isaiah declares: 'The Holy God shows himself holy in righteousness' (Isa. 5.16 RSV). Finally, that holy-righteousness was not to express itself in a mere pietistic concern for its own relationship to God. Israel, the Covenant people, was to be a kingdom of priests. A priest is ordained to serve others, not himself. The Covenant which God made with Israel at Sinai was not primarily for the good of Israel herself. The jealousy of Israel that lies behind the well-known saying 'How odd of God to choose the Jews' rests upon a misunderstanding of God's action in choosing Israel, as we read of it in the Bible. Israel is chosen by God at Sinai to be the instrument that he can use in order that *all* nations may come to know of his purpose for them. 'Let my son go, that he may *serve* me' (Ex. 4.23) says God to Pharaoh, and that service is to be the service of the whole world.

It is unfortunately only too clear from the record that few Israelites understood their calling in this light. The great prophets have therefore to make it part of their task to remind Israel of what God's promises entail. Isaiah, for example, recognizes that the promise given to Abraham, viz., that his descendants would be a blessing to the world, would come about when Israel should teach both Egypt and Assyria to worship her God (Isa. 19.23-25). The writer of Isa. 42.6 and 49.6, who lived with his fellow-exiles in far-off Babylonia after the destruction of Jerusalem in 587 BC, distinguishes God's purpose in sending Israel to Babylon as a missionary one, and evidently expects the Israelites to make individual converts (Isa. 44.1-5). The whole purpose of the book of Jonah is to recall Israel to her responsibility to

Nineveh, the great city of the East that represented pagan civilization at its most powerful.

At the same time we are to keep continually in mind that it is not merely 'Israel after the flesh' with whom God entered into covenant relationship at Mount Sinai. The people gathered at the foot of that mountain were by no means only Hebrews related to each other by blood. We are told that a 'mixed multitude' was with the Hebrews as they came out of Egypt (Ex. 12.38), and that later many native Canaanites remained to live amongst the newly-settled tribes of Israel, and to share in their national life. The Hebrews regularly intermarried with such people, as we can see from the foreign names that they bear. The little book of Ruth was written to remind the post-exilic community of Ezra's day that the great King David, God's choice of monarch for the 'special people', had a pagan Moabitess for a great-grandmother, of whom he had no need to be ashamed (Ruth 4.13, 21-22). It is probable that the majority of the inhabitants of Galilee in New Testament times were originally Gentiles who had adopted Judaism as their religion for reasons both good and bad. And St Paul insists that the promise which God gave to Abraham was not meant merely for his descendants as a racial group, for if such had been the case, then the descendants of Esau would have shared equally with the descendants of his brother Jacob in the fulfilment of the promise (Rom. 9.6-15).

God did not give the 'Law' to a people whom he intended to segregate from the world. Rather the Law is bound up with God's intention that his people should be 'his salvation unto the end of the earth' (Isa. 49.6); and his people is, equally obviously, not just the Hebrews as a racial unit. 'They are not all Israel, which are of Israel' (Rom. 9.6). So St Paul can interpret the facts of the Old Testament narrative.

3

The Content of the Law

WHAT then of the *content* of the Law which God 'gave' to Israel, his Covenant People, whether through the lips of Moses, or later when the earlier codes were carefully 'deduced' to meet new situations and new economic circumstances? Perhaps our eyes will open in surprise when we examine some of its items in detail, if we have been under the impression that the Mosaic Law was primarily concerned with ritual.

At all the three stages to which we have referred, viz., the pre-monarchical period, the period influenced by the great prophets, and the post-exilic summing-up of the whole body of the Law, we find incisive and deeply understanding items, that speak right home, not just to those for whom the Law was formed, but also to us today. Let us begin with the question of slavery.

The institution of slavery was accepted by all ancient peoples. St Paul accepted it in the New Testament. Europe accepted it till recent times. No one imagined that slavery was inherently evil in itself, any more than other forms of society are, such as the rule of the tribal chief in Africa, of the medieval baron in France, or of the chief of a Scottish clan. But by the very nature of the case the institution of slavery could be intolerable for the slave. Israel herself had learned that fact when she was still a slave in the land of Egypt, and had groaned under the lash of the taskmaster. Now, if we turn to the very early Code which we call for convenience 'the book of the Covenant' (Ex. 20-23), we find a most interesting fact. Almost at once, after the Ten Commandments have been transcribed and commented on, the Code turns to the plight of the slave in ancient Hebrew society. In other words, this Code is concerned, as is the whole Bible, with the poor and needy, the helpless, the downtrodden and unfortunate amongst men.

Ex. 21 shows us a new approach to the question of slavery. We find that no Hebrew freeman could own absolutely the person of a fellow-Hebrew, or buy and sell him as he pleased. In other words, even in early times the Hebrew view of the relationship that should obtain between master and slave, while economically necessary before other forms of society were known, was to be one of respect between *persons*. Under the influence of this law, the slave was given the status of a person as much as was his master. This meant that within Israel it was made crystal clear that the slave too had been created in the image of God. But more. He too was a member of the 'holy nation', 'the kingdom of priests'. He too had a share in the responsibility that all Israel bore in the face of the whole world of men. The work of society must go on and workers were needed in those days just as much as they are needed now for the tilling of the soil and the ingathering of the harvest. But the work of society must not go on at the cost of the *exploitation* of one Hebrew by another. To that end the employer could purchase a Hebrew slave for a period of six years only (Ex. 21.2). The latter's was not to be a 'life sentence'. He was to live in hope that some day soon he would be his own master again. This regulation, moreover, reacted favourably upon the slave-owner. He was restrained from uncalled-for cruelty by the knowledge that he only had a 'loan' of his slave for a period.

On the ground that the Hebrew slave was, in the last resort, a brother-made-in-the-image-of-God, the slave even had rights by law against his master. This was in complete contradiction to what Israel had known in Egypt, when the people as a whole had had no redress at all from Pharaoh or his taskmasters. What we read of in Exodus, of course, are the intolerable conditions prevailing in a 'public works' camp, not in private houses. But the Hebrews, to whom this legislation was given, would naturally see how the two systems were meant to compare. 'If a man smite his slave,' we read in Ex. 21.20, 'or his female-slave, with a rod, and he die under his hand, he shall be surely punished.' 'If a man smite the eye of his servant, or the eye of his maid, that it be destroyed, he shall let him go free for his eye's sake' (Ex. 21.26), and the same even for the loss of a tooth (v. 27). How different from the slavery of Egypt! And so we should notice that the whole 'book of the Covenant' is prefaced (Ex. 20.2) by a reminder from God that he had first delivered Israel 'out of the land of Egypt, out of the house of bondage'. A new situation had been entered. The Covenant had been imposed upon Israel *after* God had rescued his people from that terrible situation; the Law had now been given to Israel *within* the new Covenant situation. God had acted first in grace. It was he who had created the new situation. The hearts of individual Israelite men and women could in consequence now warm to the God who had redeemed them first. Their response to him was thus actually *created* by God's primary act of love. They had been taught thereby to see what love was. God had been good to them. They were now to be holy, even as he is holy. Therefore they were to treat their workers in a 'holy' or 'righteous' manner.

Such an effect upon the heart of the employer of labour was evidently expected. Ex. 21.5-6 deals with the situation where a slave is so well treated that he may *want* to serve his master devotedly to the end of his days. There might thus appear a slave who would actually make the extraordinary statement 'I love my master'.

It would be pointless to deny that in later societies, such as those of Greece and Rome, similar conditions prevailed. We know, in fact, of many slaves who were quite at home in their Roman master's employ, and who could even count upon the latter's help to rise to eminence in the world of politics or the arts. But the point we ought to see in this connection is twofold. First, Israel's legislation comes very early in the history of human society, and precedes Rome by a thousand years; and second, no other nation included within its statute book *regulations* for kindly treatment of its slaves. It is only a nation which regarded its law, not as 'dead' legalism, but as the Word of God spoken in concern for the poor amongst men, which could have thought of including such regulations in its code of laws.

It is at the second period of Israel's legislation that a still more interesting development takes place and shows itself in Israel's law. Here, too, the response on man's part is recognized to be the result of the primary act of God, when, in love, he redeemed his people from bondage to Pharaoh. The point is that the great prophets have by now interpreted the Code we have cited from Exodus, so that Israel's lawgivers are now *deducing* its items in a very wonderful manner: Deut. 15.12 f. is a re-examination of the passage to which we have referred, the one which deals with limiting slavery to a period of six years. But now, that is to say, in the sixth century BC, it has become clear that the love of God demands more than the mere keeping to the agreement that Ex. 21.2 demands. The 'book of the Covenant' reflects indeed a very deep understanding for the ancient world of the meaning of justice, even though the level it reflects is the 'eye for an eye' level (Ex. 21.24-25). Just because our Lord shows us a new level altogether, we are not to despise the

level reached in days even before David reigned. We read in
Matt. 5.38-42 as follows: 'Ye have heard that it hath been
said, An eye for an eye, and a tooth for a tooth: but I say
unto you, That ye resist not evil: but whosoever shall smite
thee on thy right cheek, turn to him the other also. And if
any man will sue thee at the law, and take away thy coat,
let him have thy cloak also. And whosoever shall compel
thee to go a mile, go with him twain. Give to him that
asketh thee, and from him that would borrow of thee turn
not thou away.' That is *deducing* the Law of Moses to a
degree Moses could never have envisaged! But more of that
later in our argument. Meantime we are to note that the
Deuteronomic Code now adds considerably to this item in
the 'Law', appearing as it does some four hundred years
after the 'book of the Covenant' in Exodus has begun to
speak of justice in the first place, and after the great eighth-
century prophets have expounded what it means for Israel
to live in a covenant relationship with the Lord, Yahweh.
When the six years of service are up, it now declares, the
master is not just to turn his poor worker loose in a hard
world with nothing but the clothes he stands up in. He has
to provide him with capital, as the Lord has prospered him,
so that the servant can set up again in life on his own and
earn his own living as his own master—and then comes the
reason for this humane exposition of the earlier Code: 'And
thou shalt remember that thou wast a bondman in the land
of Egypt, and the Lord thy God redeemed thee: therefore I
command thee this thing today.' On the other hand, if, by
any chance, the slave had not been happy, and had run
away from the man for whom he worked, he was not to be
sent back to where his work had not been congenial (Deut.
23.15-16). Once again we see how Israel understood her Law.
Its items were, in part, expressions of loving gratitude to
God for the love he had shown her first.

Moreover, 'It shall not seem hard unto thee, when thou sendest him away free from thee; for he hath been worth a double hired servant to thee.' He wouldn't have been that, of course, unless his master had treated him with loving consideration. If his master had been the usual eastern hard taskmaster, the servant would have done as little work for him as he could. So we see now the second wave of effect from God's initial act of grace. A simple, uneducated, boorish peasant now knows what it is to love and to be loyal to his human master even in the unpromising circumstances of the master-slave relationship.

The third step in the growth of meaning in this law dealing with slaves is seen in Lev. 25.39 ff. This chapter belongs to the priestly legislation that took final form only after the return from exile in Babylonia, well over a century after the promulgation of the Deuteronomic Law in 621 BC. Here we see how the grace of God has still further developed right relationships between man and man. Here it is stated that there is now to be no question of *compelling* a brother Hebrew who needs to work as a labourer to serve a master in the old slave relationship. He is now to be treated as a regular paid employee, or as a seasonal worker who hires himself to a Hebrew employer of labour for a specified period. And finally, once the impoverished individual has earned some money in service, he is to go back to his own family and family farm, because God set him there in the first place: 'For they (too) are *my* servants, which I brought forth out of the land of Egypt: they shall not be sold as bondmen.'

We think: 'How impressive this growing understanding of the original wording of the Mosaic Law must have appeared to the heathen who lived round about and within the land of Israel!' It was God's will that they should be impressed, and the Law was given in part for that purpose.

He had made Israel to be a kingdom of priests *vis-à-vis* the Gentiles. But we have no record that they *were* impressed to any degree at all.

The reason seems to be a simple one. This legislation probably remained only an ideal. We have only to read the great prophets to discover that the average Hebrew farmer seldom even attempted to live up to the high ideal contained in the Law. Amos, Isaiah, Micah, and then a century later, Jeremiah, all refer back to this ancient law as one that was not being kept, even when, first, King Hezekiah, in Isaiah's day, and then King Josiah, in Jeremiah's day, both sought to enforce it on employers of labour. Israel's influence on her neighbours broke down, in other words, at that point where her *witness* failed. She possessed a great ideal, enshrined within her Law. But the Law never fully became 'flesh', and therefore visible to the eyes of men. It remained clauses in a statute book, and little more.

We might adduce many items, especially from the Deuteronomic Code, to further our argument that in the 'Law of Moses' Israel possessed a legislation unique in the world's lawmaking. Deut. 22.8 suggests that when you give a party to your neighbours on your flat roof in the cool of the evening, you are wholly responsible for their safety and well-being! We should remember that our Lord quoted from Deuteronomy more than from any other book in the Old Testament. Chapters 22 to 25 contain many such deeply understanding items.

Deut. 22.1-3 asks the members of the Covenant People to do something very striking. It asks them to rescue a straying animal, and feed and care for it till its owner can be found. Now, other ancient codes had similar provisions for lost animals. But note this difference, how the item ends with the words: 'Thou mayest not hide thyself.' The finder was not to consider 'finding's keepings' or lazily say to himself 'Let the beast's owner come and get it', or 'Serve him right for losing it'. He was to go out of his way to restore the beast to its rightful owner safe and well. We remind ourselves that other nations could be equally kind to animals. But Israel alone believed that kindness came from God.

Deut. 22.4 tells our ancient Hebrew not to 'hide himself' from a neighbour's domestic animal that has fallen down a hole. 22.6 points out the fundamental truth that man can easily destroy a whole species of bird (as has happened to the dodo, the moa, and many another defenceless creature) if *both* the mother-bird *and* her eggs are consistently taken for food. A tiny verse like 22.10 represents a wonderful advance in man's treatment of the dumb creation. In origin it may have rested upon a taboo. But here in Deuteronomy it undoubtedly refers to consideration for one's domestic animals. An ox and an ass pull at very different tensions, and they would only exasperate and finally injure each other if they were yoked together before a plough; and how tantalizing it must be for a muzzled ox going round and round the central pole treading out the corn not to be able to bend down at intervals and have a mouthful of that corn for itself. The labourer is worthy of his hire, even if that labourer be only a dumb brute of an ox! (25.4). This is not something that Israel is vaguely feeling after in common with other nations. It is a revelation of the mind of God now embodied in her statute book.

Deut. 23.7-8 forbids hatred of one's ancestral enemy. Our modern laws contain no such commands. Again, even the elements of hygiene are attributed to God's special revelation (23.12-14). How could a man do anything unclean or indelicate when 'the Lord thy God walketh in the midst of thy camp'? The Israelites learned that it was important to

God what one did even in the privacy necessary to the physical functions of the body.

Family life was to be exalted. No Hebrew girl was ever to become a prostitute (23.17). A brother Hebrew ought to be glad that you trust him well enough to feel you are welcome to eat his produce if you are hungry. But it would be a mean thing to take from him more than you require at the moment (23.24-25).

It is possible for a man to be very unlucky and to have to sell everything he possesses bit by bit to feed his family. But there comes a point beyond which you as buyer must not go. Even the day-labourer's house is his castle. You must not push your way in and seize his property (24.10). If he owes you all he has, and has nothing left to give, stop at the mantle that is his coat by day and his blanket by night (24.13). To remove his final covering from him would be to treat him as an animal and render the ultimate indignity to one made in the image of God. Moreover, he is a family man. The family must eat. Under no circumstances are you to take the millstone on which his wife grinds corn for the family supper. It would be like taking her teapot from an old-age pensioner today. And so, while men were taught to pay their debts, and to suffer for the folly of their ways, they were also taught to respect the inner core of their neighbour's personality, and to stop short at depriving him of those basic possessions which show that a man is a man and not a beast.

And so we might continue. The seasonal labourer from amongst the Gentiles may perhaps belong to a despised race of foreigners. But he is a human soul cut off from the protection of his people when working in Israel's midst. That is why the 'Law of Moses' accords the 'stranger' the special protection of the Law (24.17). There are two similar helpless groups that need very special attention. The orphan is singled out for loving care, and the widow's case is always put with the orphan's. In no ancient society could a single woman 'earn her living' independently as she can do today. So the Mosaic Law demands that she be given special care, the kind of care that God had given to Israel when she had been helpless without any law at all to protect her in Egypt (24.17). The widow was to benefit from the calculated goodwill of all her neighbours, who were to make deliberate provision for her from their income. But even the detested foreigner, the seasonal labourer, was to share in this voluntary tax which the Hebrew farmer was to impose upon himself! (24.19-22).

We can well see the influence of a man like Amos upon the Law, if Deuteronomy can produce an item like: 'Thou shalt not have in thy bag divers weights, a great and a small. Thou shalt not have in thine house divers measures, a great and a small. But thou shalt have a perfect and just weight, a perfect and just measure shalt thou have' (25.13-15). But the last verse continues: 'that thy days may be lengthened in the land which the Lord thy God giveth thee'. God wanted to reward the honest shopkeeper with the gift which the ancient Hebrew desired more than all else, a long life. Amos had not seen honesty like this at the Bethel market. There he had noticed shopkeepers giving short measure ('making the ephah small') and overcharging their simple country customers ('making the shekel—the unit of finance, against which you weighed out your coins—great'), and generally 'falsifying the balances by deceit' (Amos 8.5). And so he declared with the vehemence of one who knew that those shopkeepers had snapped their fingers at a law which was a revelation of the very mind of the living God: 'The Lord hath sworn by the excellency of Jacob, Surely I will never forget any of their works. Shall not the land tremble for this?' (Amos 8.7-8).

Or later still again, in the third period of Israel's legislation, we find in the so-called 'Holiness Code' (which was probably compiled by the time of the Exile) such heart-searching commands as: 'Thou shalt not curse the deaf, nor put a stumblingblock before the blind.' Why? 'But shalt fear thy God: I am the Lord' (Lev. 19.14). God *cares* for the deaf and the blind, it seems

'Thou shalt not go up and down as a talebearer among thy people' (Lev. 19.16). So even gossiping is against God's law! 'Thou shalt not hate thy brother in thy heart' (Lev. 19.17). 'Thou shalt not avenge, nor bear any grudge against the children of thy people, but thou shalt love thy neighbour as thyself: *I am the Lord!*' (Lev. 19.18).

Is this then *law*—or is it something else? How can any nation legislate for the feelings in a human heart? The searching nature of this question will occupy us later.

On the other hand particularly in this Holiness Code that we have quoted, great emphasis is laid on ritual duties. We must pause for a while, then, and look at the significance of this emphasis if we are ever to understand the relationship between Law and Gospel which the Bible reveals. Thereafter we shall have to define finally what the Hebrews meant by their term *Torah*, translated as 'Law', in view of their difference of emphasis from the Greeks and Romans.

FOR FURTHER READING

Warde Fowler, *The Religious Experience of the Roman People*, 1911.
R. W. Livingstone, *The Pageant of Greece*, 1923.
G. R. Driver and J. C. Miles, *The Babylonian Laws*, 2 vols., 1952.
G. R. Driver and J. C. Miles, *The Assyrian Laws*, 1935.
E. Neufeld, *The Hittite Laws*, 1951.
S. N. Kramer, *From the Tablets of Sumer*, 1956.
D. Daube, *Studies in Biblical Law*, 1947.

4

The Ceremonial Law

THE 'Law' that God gave to Israel at Mount Sinai traditionally contained ceremonial material as well as ethical commands. When therefore we take up for consideration the difficult question of the ceremonial law, we are to remind ourselves that the same understanding of the word 'law' must apply now as is true for the kindly laws which regulated human relationships.

In the form in which they were remembered by at least 450 BC, Israel's laws were all considered to be of divine origin. The tradition of the two tablets of stone written with the finger of God which Moses brought down from Mount Sinai clearly points to such a belief. The inference is that the whole Mosaic Law, and not just the Ten Commandments, comes from God. That is why many of the collections of laws within the Pentateuch are prefaced by the words: 'And the Lord spake unto Moses, saying . . .' Or again, that is why the specifications for the building of the Tabernacle in the Wildnerness were understood to be copied from an original plan kept in heaven (Ex. 25.9, 40).

God 'spoke' all the commandments to Moses, then, including all the many laws that developed as the centuries unfolded. Now, when a man speaks to his friend, he does two things at once. He teaches him what he wants him to know, and at the same time he reveals to him what is in his own mind. The Hebrew word for 'teach' is a form of the

verb 'to shoot'. A man may shoot an arrow to show direction. Consequently the transitive form of the verb was used
for 'pointing out', 'showing the way', 'instructing', 'direct-
ing' and 'teaching'. The noun built from this verb is the
word *Torah*. The latter is actually the word used for the
'Law of Moses'. But now we see that it is far removed in
meaning from either the Latin *lex* or the Greek *nomos*, that
in fact it means both 'instruction' and 'revelation', and does
not contain the idea of legalism in it at all. Moreover,
fundamentally it implies a personal relationship between
the teacher and the taught, between the revealer and the
one to whom the latter reveals his mind. The Hebrew word
for law thus takes on meaning in a situation only such as
we have outlined, such as where we have a covenant relationship between a people and their living and personal
God.

As the years went by, and as this unique relationship developed, Israel grew to know more and more of the mind
of God. Her priests continued to 'give *torah*' so as to meet
the varying new situations that arose as year succeeded year.
Israel's economic life developed. We can read in I Kings how
complicated her society had become even by the end of Solomon's reign in comparison with the simple agrarian society
which marked her civilization when David first came to the
throne. It is very obvious to us as we read the Pentateuch
that many of those laws, of which it is said 'The Lord said
unto Moses . . .' derive from the period of, and are adapted
for, the developed civilization of the kingdom. But it was
not only economically that Israel grew. Under the guidance
of the great prophets, and at the hand of many an unknown
local priest and unnamed cultic prophet, Israel's knowledge
of what God required of her in relationship to himself deep-
ened beyond all measure.

We have seen how a man's understanding of his duties to

his brother and sister Hebrew grew as the years went by, that growth being recorded in each successive level of legislation as it was made. But a parallel was also being made in the realm of ritual. Israel's ritual was her attempt to act out in practice that personal relationship which she ought to have with Yahweh. Her ritual, with all her many sacrifices and festivals, was meant to be the formulation of a people's response in gratitude and loyalty, within the covenant relationship, to a God who had laid it upon her that a ritual is necessary if fellowship with himself is to be maintained. Israel's sacrifices, therefore, were truly 'means of grace' by the practice of which she both kept in touch with Yahweh her Lord and received the assurance of his pardoning love and power. Yet, of course, we must at once admit that we speak here once again only of the ideal. The Old Testament itself reveals to us with blinding clarity that the ordinary Israelite was constantly rebelling against the Law of God as it was taught him by his priests. Be that as it may, the priestly writings contain a codification of laws that have to do in large measure with the ritual which had developed up to the century succeeding the return from Exile, i.e. from 540 BC onwards. They contain, for example, the Code of Holiness' (Lev. 17-26) which comprises material that was taking shape even before the Exile began. And the priestly writings comment on and develop laws concerning ritual that go back even to the days of Moses.

But, as we have seen, Isaiah had taught his people a new meaning to the word 'holy'. If Israel was indeed to be Yahweh's *segullah*, his precious possession, then she too must be holy, even as God himself is holy. These words form a refrain that recurs frequently within the priestly material. 'For I am the Lord that bringeth you up out of the land of Egypt, to be your God.' We have noticed before this emphasis upon the primary act of grace on God's part. But now the priestly phrase continues: 'Ye shall therefore be holy, for I am holy.'

In consequence of this command, everything to do with Israel's ritual had to be made holy too. In early days, the concept of holiness was indeed a primitive notion, as primitive as the notions of *mana* and *tapu* amongst the Maoris of New Zealand. But Israel's priests, following the lead of Isaiah, were able now to put new content into the word.

First of all, heathen practices were now condemned as never before (cf. Lev. 19.19, 26-29, 31), and men who did not belong to the 'holy people' were granted no access to Israel's worship. Necromancy (Lev. 20.6-8, 27), unchastity (Lev. 20.10-21), incestuous marriages (Lev. 18.6 ff.), and such-like, were wholly forbidden to the 'holy' people. A special priesthood, rendered 'holy' by a certain prescription, and kept 'holy' by obedience to certain new laws (cf. Lev. 21.1-9, 16-24) was set in charge of Israel's sacrifices. Certain foods were considered 'holy' both for human consumption and for God's use on the altar (Lev. 22.21 ff.). Here indeed, if nowhere else, we are aware of (1) a strong dependence upon ancient taboos, and (2) reaction against disgusting observances of the Canaanites. Certain days were set aside as holy, the great festivals for example (Lev. 23.4-25), but especially the Sabbath day (Lev. 23.1-3). Even the very utensils for use at the sacrifices were to be rendered 'holy', and objects vowed to Yahweh, tithes and devoted things, each in turn entered the sphere of the holy when they were dedicated to the service of Yahweh.

Such, of course, is a mere sketch of a very complicated development in Israel's life, for we have only to read the second half of the book of Exodus, all of the book of Leviticus, and much of the book of Numbers, to see how the realm of the holy was continually being enlarged until great areas of the life of the People of God were brought within its sphere. It is not attractive to us that Israel at this time laid such emphasis on the sanctifying of *things*. Yet by this means she sought to obey the command to be holy even as God is holy. The care of *things* gave her a field of service where she believed she did his will. We ought to notice the significant fact, therefore, before we approach the question of the relevance of these laws for our own day (or, rather, irrelevance, as we shall see later), that the pious Israelite in the period soon after the return from Exile regarded the keeping of the laws promulgated in the Holiness Code and elsewhere as no burden upon him at all. On the contrary, recognizing that it was the God of the Covenant relationship who had given them to Israel in the first place, and that these laws had been 'revealed' by Yahweh for his own good and the good of his fellow-Israelite, the thoughtful and pious member of the Covenant People could declare with vehemence and sincerity: 'O how love I thy law! it is my meditation all the day' (Ps. 119.97). We have only to read right through the long 119th Psalm to discover how fundamental to his joy and peace of mind the Law was, if he could declare in that Psalm (v. 105) 'Thy word is a lamp unto my feet, and a light unto my path'. The Law was no burden upon his shoulders to be borne with resignation—it was *Torah*; it was the final revelation of the mind of the living God, who through the marvellous relationship which he planned to produce with his chosen people, whom he guided by the precepts of the *Torah*, would one day redeem the whole earth, and win all men home to his love and care.

The Psalmist multiplies words in his ecstatic praise of the Law. 'I esteem all thy precepts' (v. 128); 'thy testimonies are wonderful' (v. 129); 'the entrance of thy words giveth light' (v. 130); 'I longed for thy commandments' (v. 131); 'O Lord, I will keep thy statutes' (v. 145); 'consider how I love thy

precepts . . . the sum of thy word is truth, and every one
of thy righteous ordinances endures for ever' (vv. 159-160
RSV). These are the words of one who clearly sees *why* God
has laid his Covenant upon Israel, and where the Law fits
into that covenant relationship. In a word, the 'revelation'
and 'instruction' (some of which may indeed appear to be
legal *formulae*) that are the content of *Torah*, the Law, are
to be understood in terms quite different from the various
words for 'law' in other languages, and only as an essential
element in the total Covenant relationship by which Israel
was bound to the God who had redeemed her in the first
place from the bondage of Egypt.

As we said above, parallel with the developing understanding of God's ways with his chosen people there went a
development of worship and its accompanying ritual. The
truth of this becomes very evident in the post-exilic period,
and for obvious reasons. The priestly and prophetic interpreters of God's ways with Israel were seeking to dramatize
these for the ordinary worshipper. The issue is noticeable
in the book of Ezekiel, then again in Isaiah 40-55, both of
which saw the light in the Babylonian exile. Moreover, in
Isaiah 56-66 the issue is raised again for that generation
which had to face the hard realities of life as it tried to
reconstitute its nationhood in what remained of the once
beautiful city of Jerusalem, after it had returned from exile
in 538 BC. These prophets wrestle with the problem as to
what God was meaning when he allowed Israel to suffer the
loss of Jerusalem in 587 BC, and permitted the break-up of
the nation as an economic and political entity; and what
Israel's suffering in exile meant in the light of the Covenant
relationship which bound her to her God. Now, since the
Pentateuch was finalized only after these interpreters had
made their significant contributions, their 'findings', so to
speak, became part of the dramatization of God's saving

activity right as far back as the time of the Exodus, and were integrated into the ceremonial legislated for in the Pentateuchal 'law'. This is an important point to remember. The ceremonial law is in part actually an interpretation of God's saving and recreative love for Israel and for the world. Let us note then what the prophets did actually discover God had been doing in their chequered history.

They believed that the Exile (when Nebuchadnezzar in 587 BC carried off the cream of Jerusalem's population to Babylonia) was God's punishment for Israel's apostasy from fellowship and co-operation with the God who had chosen her in love. But more. The sufferings of the Exile were (a) purgative in their efficacy and thus recreative for Israel's life; God was forgiving Israel all her sins by sharing with her all the sufferings, both mental and physical, that she had had to go through. He was doing so by inviting her to take his yoke upon her, and learn of him; God was thus bearing her sins and carrying her sorrows, as a good husband would surely do for his beloved. In this way God won for Israel forgiveness, renewal and the chance to begin again. That is how Israel was in the position to return to Jerusalem and reconstitute her life there once again under God when the Exile came to an end. (b) The sufferings of Israel were now seen to take their place within the original purpose of the Covenant given at Sinai. There, we recall, Israel had been summoned to become a kingdom of priests towards the Gentiles. Now God had accepted Israel's sufferings, begun though they had been as penal, and much deserved as they were in fact, and had brought those sufferings also within the sphere of the Covenant. Thus a new vista now opened up in the interpretation of God's Covenant with Israel. Israel's sufferings within the Covenant were meant to render her a light to lighten the Gentiles! (Isa. 49.5-6). God's Word of love and concern was to be made

known to those *outside* the Covenant by means of the suffering of his people; and the Gentiles were to be *brought in*
within the fellowship of the Covenant to share in Israel's joy
through the extraordinary medium of the willing offering
of a people united in purpose with the God of all the earth!
(Isa. 49.8, 18; 60.3-22).

The fact of the Exile did more than anything else in
Israel's experience since the days of Moses to show her the
ways of God for the world. What had seemed like the ultimate tragedy—the destruction of the Temple and the end
of Jerusalem, the scattering of Israel to the winds, the evident frustration of the plans of God for Israel and the nulli-
fying of all the promises God had made through his
Covenant with the Patriarchs and his Covenant given
through Moses—all this was a tragedy no more. Out of the
pain and suffering and frustration of the seeming destruction of his Covenant People God had produced his method
for saving the world!

We can well believe that only a few choice souls within
Israel were able to think their way through to an understanding of this fundamental truth. But some of those who
did must have belonged to the line of priests who were
descended from other priests who had served at the Jerusalem Temple in the days before Nebuchadnezzar had performed his fell task as God's instrument to punish his
people (see Jer. 25.9, where God calls Nebuchadnezzar 'my
servant'). This we believe to be the case, on the ground that
in the post-exilic period new legislation arose in connection
with the cult which sought to reflect this new depth of
understanding of the ways of God with Israel.

We are to remember that the priests brought back from
Exile a large part of the legal material that now comprises
our Pentateuch. They obviously possessed all that noble
legislation which is to be found in Deut. 12-26, 28. Much of

this, as we have seen, is a development of earlier material now found in our book of Exodus. These sources contain both ethical commandments and legal enactments such as are necessary for the conduct and welfare of society in both war and peace. But they also include ritual commands. One of the oldest sources that we possess we call for convenience 'the Ritual Decalogue'. It is to be found within Ex. 34. The question of clean and unclean meats is to be found in Deut. 14.

Now, it is just this ritual element that was primarily developed in the post-exilic period, and which is one of the chief interests of the priestly literature. Thus, for example, the elaborate details we possess in Exodus of the structure of the Tabernacle come from the pen of this priestly school. Moreover, although the priestly writing is comparatively late, it is the true descendant of early primitive notions. We cannot gainsay the fact that many of the lesser sacrifices and ritual practices of Israel are little different from the sacrifices and practices of the Canaanites who were their neighbours over the years. Some of the developed ceremonial laws, in fact, are little more than vestigial remains of primitive and pagan acts. The realization of the futility of certain of Israel's inherited practices and ceremonies must therefore have come home to the minds of that loyal group of exiled Israelites, of whom we have spoken. As they witnessed their Babylonian masters performing ceremonial acts in honour of, or in order to placate, their particular conception of the divine beings, thoughtful Israelites must have become vividly aware that many of these actions were very similar to theirs. But they had also become aware that *their* Temple was now in ruins and far away. Yet despite that fact they knew that they still possessed in exile the presence of the living God just as fully and meaningfully as ever they did in Jerusalem in days of old.

After the return from exile, however, the priestly element in the community reconstituted the sacrificial and ceremonial worship, and introduced practices that were growing ever more and more complicated. The most significant of the post-exilic rituals, however, that for the Day of Atonement, an account of which may be discovered in Lev. 16, has an importance in the cult above all the others that Israel seems now to have been blindly following. The Epistle to the Hebrews in the New Testament concerns itself with this ritual of the Day of Atonement on the ground that it is the typical form of Jewish sacrifice, and thus representative of them all.

To discuss the ritual of the Day of Atonement in detail is more than we need to do now. It will be sufficient for us to note its main emphases. The ceremony was instituted in the post-exilic period, so far as we know, in order to meet a felt need on the part of Israel. She needed to appropriate every year over again that forgiveness which God had offered and declared to her at the end of the period of the Exile (see Isa. 40.1). In that period God had shown that forgiveness was more than just a shrugging off on his part of Israel's sins. Forgiveness involved his own suffering. Forgiveness meant that he had taken upon himself the judgment he had meted out to Israel's sin, and borne it away himself. By means of this annually conducted ritual, therefore, Israel sought to re-present the atonement which God had wrought, when, united as one with his people, God had shown her what it meant to become the Suffering Servant that would take away the sins of the world. There is just a hint, but a most significant hint, that in the last resort it is God himself who has been the real scapegoat of the exile period: 'I did not impose the office of the Servant upon *you*,' says God to Israel, '. . . it was you who made *me* the Servant (who dealt) with your sins, and who made *me* toil over your iniquities' (Isa. 43.23-24). This verse is not elaborated; we are just left with this astounding verse uttered by the same individual who has drawn for us the portrait of the Suffering Servant in Isa. 53. In the Day of Atonement ritual, accordingly, a goat (sc. a *scape*-goat) bore away Israel's sin into the wilderness. Then finally, emphasis is to be placed on the fact that it was the High Priest who performed the ritual on this great and important day in Israel's year. Yet for that day alone he wore the same clothes as the other priests. He did this in order to signify that he was in no sense different from or 'above' them in office; he was the first among equals. Yet the Old Testament priesthood was merely one section of the nation as a whole, and was neither different from, nor 'above', the Israelites whom it represented. Thus the action of the High Priest in the course of the sacrifice, in entering within the veil, and in driving the scapegoat away into the desert, was performed with the object that *all Israel* might once more recover its proper status before God as a kingdom of priests, forgiven and renewed and cleansed, and thus be able to bear the task of mediating the knowledge and love of God to the Gentiles.

The Day of Atonement ritual is thus by no means meaningless, even if we accept the fact that some of the other ritual acts had probably little to say to educated Jews in the centuries immediately before the coming of Christ. The so-called 'Wisdom literature' in the Old Testament—books like Proverbs and Job, along with other inter-testamental literature, some of which is to be found in the Apocrypha—pays scant attention to the whole sacrificial system and to the ceremonial law. While the argument from silence is not conclusive, yet this fact would suggest that many of the 'intellectuals' amongst the Jews were looking elsewhere than to the ceremonial laws for satisfaction and for fellowship with God. Such may well have been true even for the Day of Atonement ritual, even though the Epistle to the Hebrews takes it for granted that this annual ceremony was central to the cult.

In AD 70 the Romans destroyed the Temple in Jerusalem for the last time. The ritual that had developed from the days of Moses was never performed again. On the one hand it could be said that the ritual had now made itself unnecessary, and that it had lost its *raison d'être* as mere ritual and ceremonial now that men had learned from experience what it was meant to portray. On the other hand, the theological significance which it latterly sought to dramatize was no longer necessarily bound to those particular ceremonial acts. At least so thought the early Christian Church. For it believed that the reality which the ceremonial law dramatized was now fulfilled in a new dimension in the Cross and Resurrection of Christ.[1]

[1] See A. S. Herbert, *Worship in Ancient Israel*, 1959.

5

The Meaning of *Torah*

WE are now confronted with the interesting fact that by New Testament times there had appeared amongst Jewry at least two interpretations of the word *Torah*. First there was the legalistic emphasis which we find that Ezra was able to impose upon his contemporaries, and which remained to be the prime emphasis in later years. This legalism, however, has its roots as far back as the period of the great prophets, and is obviously the object of concern by these great men. This emphasis declared itself in two ways:

(a) It required segregation of Israel from the world. We have no right from our vantage point to condemn Ezra for his actions in this regard. In all probability his was the only possible thing to do for the period in which he lived. The middle of the fifth century BC, when Ezra was active, was almost a hundred years after the return from exile. The reconstituted city of Jerusalem, with its few miles round about, was tiny in comparison with the vast Persian empire to which it belonged as a vassal dependency. Thus the unique faith of its people might quite possibly have lost its distinctive nature, faced as it was by a natural syncretism of the many faiths of the empire. Ezra may in fact have done the only right thing for his day when he 'put a hedge round the Law', and turned Israel into 'the people of the Law'. It may therefore have been necessary in the circumstances for Ezra to insist that the citizens of Jerusalem

should divorce their foreign wives (Ezra 10), as a practical
expedient for that moment in history. But the effect upon
Jewish belief in later years was such as to induce Israel to
exalt blood-relationship as that which set her apart from
her neighbours. We have seen that neither the prophets nor
St Paul accepted this conception of Israel as the true one in
God's sight.

(b) It required an emphasis upon legalism. The spiritual
descendants of Ezra now ignored the prophetic interpretation which we have seen is intertwined with the legal element to be found in the *Torah*. The insight that Israel was
called of God to be his servant, to be a light to lighten the
Gentiles, and thus not to be concerned first with her own
salvation and preservation, was relegated to the background.
So, too, was the theological interpretation of Israel's past
that the latest components of the Pentateuch regard as of
prime significance. Instead, the Rabbis laid emphasis upon
the 613 'laws' which they were able to deduce from the
Pentateuch, and which they employed as a framework for
the conduct of the whole of life. The 'oral law', out of which
the Pharisees answered Jesus in the Gospel stories, is evidence that this pattern was forming as early as the first
century, although the legalistic deduction from the *Torah*
was not codified and given written form till later centuries.

New Testament scholarship has made us aware that the
Fourth Gospel was the last of the four to be written. Its
author, at the end of the first Christian century, was meeting
with a Judaism that had hardened into a mould such as we
have outlined above. Judaism had adopted by then a legalistic position which was the direct outcome of Ezra's earlier
reformation, and which at the same time was a reaction
against the very differently orientated Christian faith with
which it was now significantly challenged. This later Judaism
is obviously that which is represented by that group which

the Fourth Gospel calls 'the Jews'. They stand in opposition
to Jesus' interpretation of the Law to a degree that is not
apparent in the earlier Synoptic Gospels (cf. John 2.18; 3.25;
5.10; 6.41, 52; etc.). Moreover, theirs was that view of the
Torah which the Fourth Gospel could place in opposition
to the 'grace' that came into the world in Christ.

On the other hand, we have seen that *Torah* could carry
a much wider, deeper and fuller significance for the contemporaries of Jesus than that which is apparent at a later
period in St John's Gospel. In the Old Testament itself,
Torah could be applied to material that is not legislative in
nature at all. For example, since the word *Torah* means
both 'teaching' and 'revelation', the great prophets made use
of it to describe their own inspired words, as they believed
them to be. 'This is a rebellious people', says Isaiah, 'children that will not hear the *Torah* of the Lord' (Isa. 30.9).
'Bind up the testimony,' he says, 'seal the teaching (*Torah*)
among my disciples' (Isa. 8.16 RSV). Here is a specific instance where *Torah* is not in the form of legal enactments.
Again, the task of the Servant in Isa. 42.4 is to take *Torah*,
or God's Word, to the far-off coast lands of the Mediterranean. Here the word seems to be synonymous with the
whole field of revelation, and to be the whole story of God's
creative act in calling Israel to be his people, and so to be
his servant and priest to the Gentile nations. The call of
Israel in the days of Moses, the call of Moses himself at the
burning bush, are now illumined by the presence of God
with Israel in the 'fires' of the Exile experience. 'When thou
walkest through the fire, thou shalt not be burned; neither
shall the flame kindle upon thee' (Isa. 43.2). This promise
Israel had now found to be true, and thus could understand
the truth of a similar experience through which Moses had
gone so long before.

We may now take the next step, and remind ourselves

that if the narrative dealing with the Exodus is *Torah*, then so also are the contents of the book of Genesis. This is because the word *Torah*, by New Testament times, means the whole first five books of the Old Testament, and cer-tainly not just the legal element within them, even when the word *Torah* is translated into the Greek of the New Testament period by the word *nomos*. The promises given to the Patriarchs are thus part of *Torah*; so is the rich and deep purpose unfolding in the adventures of Joseph. But even more important is it to recognize that the first Chris-tian century deemed the stories of Creation, of the Fall, and of Noah's Flood, to be part of *Torah*. The stories of Adam, Noah, and the Tower of Babel, all reveal to us the wicked-ness of the human heart, the fallen nature of man, and thus reveal the need for a divine action if man is to be redeemed at all from the state in which he finds himself. *Torah* sees the call of Israel to be the son of God (Ex. 4.22) as that divine action in its first stage.

The post-exilic editors of the *Torah* thus clearly recog-nized the first five books of the Old Testament to be more than a mere deposit of truth in legal form, meant to be deduced to suit every possible contingency in human life. Rather they saw it as a growing revelation of God's ways in the past that acted as a guide for understanding his will for the future, as he led his people by the Spirit into ever deeper knowledge of what that will demanded of them.[1]

Now, amongst the many other items mentioned above, the conception of the 'Covenant' is to be found within the *Torah*.

[1] See H. M. J. Loewe, *The Place of the Law in Modern Jewish Teaching*, in 'In Spirit and in Truth', 1934, pp. 229 ff.; H. J. Schoeps, *Faith and the Jewish Law Today*, in 'The Church and the Jewish People', 1954, pp. 63 ff.

6

Jeremiah's New Covenant

JEREMIAH lived in Jerusalem at that terrible time when the Babylonians were swiftly and easily conquering the whole of the Levant right down to the border of Egypt. He recognized that the doom coming on Jerusalem was deserved, and he lived to see that doom fall. All the law-keeping, all the punctilious observance of the ritual at the altar at the Temple, had failed to placate an angry God, it would seem, and the ritual of the cult of Yahweh came to an end.

As that day of doom drew near, however, Jeremiah made plain to his friends an exciting understanding he had reached of the purpose of God despite all appearances to the contrary. The first Covenant of which Jeremiah's countrymen were so proud, the Covenant that God had made with Israel at Mount Sinai, might seem to be of no avail, on the ground that Israel had not kept her part of the bargain. She had not obeyed God's voice (Ex. 19.5). It was clear then to Jeremiah, and to those who shared his insights, that the judgment of God must therefore necessarily fall. But God's judgment and his mercy are not two things, but one. That truth Jeremiah came to understand in the bitterness of his own personal experience. The judgment, in the shape of the destruction of Jerusalem, the end of the Temple worship, and the carrying away of Jerusalem's inhabitants into exile, were events that would all take place in the short space of a few months. But that judgment, Jeremiah came to see,

would in itself be a mercy. The fate that was to befall
Jerusalem would be the one thing that would save her from
the wrong understanding and appreciation she held of the
Covenant relationship which bound her to Yahweh, and
thus from the wrong conception she held of the place of the
Law in her daily life. It could only be the destruction of the
old notions that could allow the right notions to come home
to Israel's heart. New wine cannot be put into old wine-
skins. God accounted the right understanding of the Law
and of the Covenant so fundamentally important that he
was prepared even to put an end to the situation in which
Israel rejoiced, if thereby he could win her to what she was
meant to know of his purpose. He was prepared to let her
suffer the 'death' of the Exile if by that means she could
gain the new life he meant her to have. That new life was
to be found only in right relationships to the 'living' God.
Once Israel understood this, then, said Jeremiah, God would
enter into a *new* Covenant, 'not according to the covenant
that I made with their fathers . . . but . . . I will put my
law in their inward parts, and write it in their hearts; and
will be their God, they shall be my people . . . and they
shall all know me' (Jer. 31.31-34). So let us look more closely
at the actual phraseology used by Jeremiah.

Firstly we are to recognize the poverty of the English
language where it uses the simple word 'new'. French, Ger-
man, and Greek have each two words where we have one.
The word 'new' in English can mean 'completely different',
or it can mean 'renewed'. Jeremiah's Hebrew word means
this second thing. We know that the author of Hebrews 8.8-11
thought so anyway, because he used there the Greek word
that bears this meaning, and which occurs in the Septuagint
translation of this passage of Jeremiah that he is quoting.
The Hebrew root normally bears the conception of 'renew'.
It is used in the Old Testament of restoring temples, of re-

building cities, and suchlike—always, be it noted, of *re-newing that which is already there* (cf. Ps. 51.10; 104.30; Isa. 61.4; Lam. 5.21; II Chron. 15.8; 24.4; and in another form of the verb, Ps. 103.5). It is the same word in essence as the word for 'new moon'. The moon renews itself every month. But it is the *same moon* that does so; the new moon is not a 'new' moon, one that is different from the moon that appeared the month before. Similarly with the adjective from the same root. The new thing that God is about to do in Isa. 43.19; 48.6, that is, bring about a 'new Exodus', this time from the land of Babylonia, has meaning only because it will take shape on the basis of the old Exodus in the days of Moses. Ezekiel's words 'I will make you a new heart' (Ezek. 18.31; 36.22) have meaning only for hearers who already possess a heart. This understanding of the word 'new' is visible similarly in such phrases as 'Sing unto the Lord a new song' (Ps. 33.3; 96.1), or 'I will create new heavens and a new earth' (Isa. 65.17; 66.22). Naturally there are occasions, as a good concordance will show, where the one and only adjective in Hebrew for 'new' has to serve in several capacities; but the verbal root undoubtedly possesses only the meaning we suggest.[1]

Secondly, we are told quite distinctly with whom this Covenant was to be made. It was not to be with the Moabites, or the Romans, or the Irish. Nor was it to be with you and me. It was to be 'with the house of Israel, and with the house of Judah'; in other words, with the Jews. Thirdly,

[1] See Kittel, *Theologisches Wörterbuch zum Neuen Testament*, III, p. 452, article by Behm. The writer shows that the word *kainos* (new), which is used in the New Testament to translate the word 'New' Covenant, in classical Greek meant just what it means here, while *neos* (also meaning 'new') was there reserved for what is wholly and originally new. On the other hand, the phrase *he palaia diatheke* (the Old Covenant) occurs only once in the whole New Testament (II Cor. 3.14), where it undoubtedly just emphasizes that the Old Covenant is 'ancient'.

there is no suggestion that the old Law which God had
given Israel through Moses had had its day, so that God
would scrap the old one and give Israel a new one. The first
Law was God's Law. When God makes this new Covenant
therefore he will not disown his own Law! That would be
absurd. What he will do will be to write the old Law in the
hearts of his people. It is true that Heb. 7.12 speaks of
the Law being 'changed' (and we shall discuss this later).
But in saying so it does not suggest that the new Covenant
will need along with it a new law, a newly written law, a law
that supersedes the old Law given at Sinai. That idea is not
to be found in the Bible. Jer. 31.34 continues: '. . . and
they shall teach no more every man his neighbour, and
every man his brother, saying, Know the Lord: for they
shall all know me, from the least of them unto the greatest
of them, saith the Lord: for I will forgive their iniquity,
and I will remember their sin no more'.

Let us note two important points arising from this quotation:

(a) *All* Israel 'on that day' (the day when God will act in
a special way) will 'know' the Lord. This new situation
obviously cannot be brought about by sinful Israel. No
group of sinful men can act in such a manner that they
bring about a result that is a hundred per cent effective.
The coming action must be performed by God alone.

(b) Israel will then *know* the Lord. This is Hosea's word,
which he had used a century before (cf. Hos. 4.6), and which
Jeremiah adopts just as he shows his indebtedness to Hosea
elsewhere too. Hosea used it to describe the deep fellowship
that a man and his wife may have together. The verb thus
covers all possible aspects of 'knowing', mental, moral and
physical alike (cf. Gen. 4.1). Although we employ this ex-
planation of 'knowing' only as a metaphor, we can be
aghast at the implications of the word. Thus, once again, it

can be God alone who will bring about this revolution in
divine-human relationships for *all Israel* to *know* him in
this sense. Israel cannot do this thing for herself. The pain-
ful abscesses on the body of Israel (cf. Isa. 1.6) cannot be
cured by lancing them from without. The blood-stream
within must be cleansed by the renewing of the heart,
which is of course the animating and regulating centre of
the body. Israel must first then receive a new heart before
she can ever 'know' God in this vital and wonderful way.
And with that, of course, is bound up the whole question of
the forgiveness of sins, because without an act of forgiveness, no such fellowship can possibly come about.

Yet we are faced with the anomaly that the Law given at
Sinai was meant to do just exactly this for Israel. Even ob-
scure and seemingly irrelevant injunctions contributed to
this end, such as those that deal with the construction and
furnishings of the Tabernacle, and which specify exactly
what offerings were to be made to God at the door of the
Tabernacle. Now, those instructions conclude with the
words: '. . . and I will dwell among the children of Israel,
and will be their God. And *they shall know that I am the
Lord their God*, that brought them forth out of the land of
Egypt, that I may dwell among them: I am the Lord their
God' (Ex. 29.45-46).

Jeremiah must therefore be affirming his faith in the
promises of God, and seeing the Law given at Sinai as only
the first step towards this great experience of 'knowing' God.
The point is that the Old Testament contains promises
made by God, rather than prophecies made by man. Moreover, the Old Testament writers can conceive of those
promises being fulfilled only on the basis of what God has
already done in Israel's history. Now, it is the *Torah* which
tells us what God has already done; and since God is 'faithful', that is, consistent with himself, then the new Covenant

that he will make 'on that day' will be based securely upon the old one which is, of course, no less than the Word of the Lord.

We are to remember that the priestly material contained in the *Torah* was not available to Jeremiah in written form. But that does not mean that he had no access to other important interpretations of the Creation, the Fall, and the Promise given to Abraham, as well as of the whole Exodus-Sinai nexus of events, for the oral tradition behind them is already visible in the traditions that we call J and E. Without entering into discussion of this issue, it is enough for us to realize that Jeremiah and his contemporaries were well aware of Yahweh's initial purpose in choosing Israel from out of all the nations of the earth, and in giving her her Law. Consequently we are to keep in the forefront of our understanding of Jeremiah's use of the covenant idea his awareness that the Covenant made at Sinai was in some sense incomplete, and therefore but a firstfruits of something still to come.[1]

[1] See H. Cunliffe-Jones, *Jeremiah*, 1960.

7

'The Law . . . Grace and Truth'

SEEN in this great and wide context which we have described, it is clear that the giving of *Torah* is both a promise and an act of grace on God's part. What then is grace, and does John 1.17 mean that grace was unknown before the coming of Christ? That cannot be so, since grace is an Old Testament word. Thus it would be wrong to suggest that 'grace and truth' *first* came only by Jesus of Nazareth. Grace came in the Garden of Eden; grace came to Noah before the Flood; it came to Abraham when, as an unworthy heathen, God condescended to call him to be his instrument. Grace, of course, is a word which signifies the *undeserved* love of a compassionate God. We should realize, moreover, that the idea can be found more frequently in the Old Testament than we might imagine, since it sometimes hides itself under the guise of the English word 'favour'. On the other hand, grace clearly assumed a new dimension in the revelation of God which we have received in Christ, and in the redemption of the world which he wrought by Christ's death and resurrection. But here once again we must use the word 'new' as we have found it to be used in the whole Bible. The grace which came by Jesus Christ is not wholly other than the grace that God showered upon Israel in days of old. If that were indeed the case, then God would not be consistent with himself; he would not be the 'faithful', the 'reliable' God that the Old Testament speaks about. What we have received in Christ is the same grace as of old, renewed 'to the nth degree'. In other words, it is the old grace fulfilled, or 'filled full'. Yet this 'filled-full' grace is *so* great and *so* comprehensive that a *new* situation has now arisen. If we may anticipate the argument, a full cup presents us with a set of facts different from those that arise from a half-filled cup, even when the same liquid may be drunk from both. The grace that came by Jesus Christ is therefore the same grace as Moses knew, yet now knowable to a degree that Moses could never have experienced.

So too in the case of 'truth'. It too is an Old Testament word quite as much as a New Testament one. Its meaning too needs attention. The root idea behind the word for 'truth' in Hebrew is that of 'make firm', and so of 'confirming' or 'establishing'. Thus God 'confirms' or 'makes sure' the dynasty of David (II Sam. 7.16). Of course, if it is *God* who does so, then that dynasty will certainly stand, because God is reliable. God is the 'reliable', the 'trustworthy' God. These adjectives both translate the same root. He is the God on whom we can build; he is the Rock.

It is interesting that the term Rock as applied to the divine being goes back into the mists of Mesopotamian history. The Hebrews obviously believed that this ancient pictorial conception aptly fitted their understanding of the true nature of Yahweh, their God. Many a Psalmist thus addresses God as such (e.g. Ps. 18; 89); but very old passages do the same (e.g. Deut. 32), showing that the figure of Rock was used for many centuries as a valuable pictorial representation of the theological concept of Yahweh's reliability.

With this picture in mind, we are helped to see the meaning of two cognate Hebrew ideas, viz. 'truth', and 'faith'. 'Truth' is that which is firmly based upon the Rock, which is God himself. 'O send out thy light and thy truth,' says the Psalmist (Ps. 43.3); 'the truth of the Lord endureth for ever' (Ps. 117.2); 'thy law is the truth' (Ps. 119.142). In each case that we have quoted, however, this word 'truth' could be translated equally well as 'faithfulness', 'reliability', reliable because it proceeds from the reliable, trustworthy Rock that is God. Then again, 'faith' comes from the same root. The verb 'to believe' means 'to find another reliable', 'to trust in' another; and if that other be no less than Rock, then that other is reliable and trustworthy indeed. In the Old Testament, 'faith' is not primarily a subjective act or experience. It is assenting to, and so accepting, the faithfulness, the 'truth' of God, in whom one can utterly trust, since he is the Rock of ages which cannot be moved.

In modern English 'truth' is an abstract noun. A philosopher may argue about its nature; 'jesting Pilate' may show how superficial is his thought by asking 'What is truth?' (John 18.38). Yet Pilate may not have been jesting; he may have been thinking the question aloud in all sincerity. But both the philosopher and Pilate reveal that they understand the word quite differently from the way that Christ was using it. In the Old Testament 'truth' is not an abstraction at all. 'Truth' is an aspect of the nature of the living God. God reveals himself to Israel in historical situations, through concrete events, through personal relationships with individual men and women. He reveals himself thus as the 'reliable' God, and not as the abstraction that we call 'truth'. And all throughout the Old Testament we are shown men and women who come to learn the 'truth', not by intellectual ratiocination, but by placing their feet upon the Rock, and thereby finding that they are sharing in the truth of God, their trustworthy God, as he reveals his reliable nature and plan to the world. *Cogito ergo sum*, 'I think, therefore I exist', the philosopher Descartes has said in modern times. But *Crede, ut intelligas*, said St Augustine in the fifth century of our era, thereby showing a much surer grasp of the biblical conception of truth. 'Believe, *so as to* understand.' 'I set my feet on the Rock that is truth, and then in utter trust in the reliability, the trustworthiness of that Rock, I learn the truth of the universe.'

'The Law was given by Moses, but Grace and Truth came by Jesus Christ.' If at this juncture we understand by the word 'Law' the wider and deeper meaning we have found that it can contain, then the unity of the Old and the New Covenants becomes ever clearer as we proceed. Even as we overhear our Lord declaring of himself 'I am the truth' (John 14.6), if the Fourth Gospel understands aright what he must have said, then we recognize that he is making use of the same word that we have seen meant faith in the living, personal, reliable Rock of the Old Testament Covenant, who had already offered himself as the ground of all faith and truth to his chosen people, Israel.

Yet the paradox remains that in Christ this truth is also something wholly new. He alone of all men can say 'I am the truth'. Its paradoxical nature is parallel to the unique relationship that obtains between the two Covenants. In the words of the institution of the new Covenant, as they have been delivered to us by St Paul (I Cor. 11.25), we find an explicit reference to the phrase *he kaine diatheke* (i.e. 'the new covenant') that Jeremiah used (Jer. 31.31; or 38.31 in the Septuagint translation). The word *kaine* (new) in this quotation therefore must necessarily refer to the renewal of the old Covenant as the latter finds its fulfilment in the unrepeatable work of Christ upon the Cross. This means that in his new Covenant, Christ is reaffirming but at the same time clinching, so to speak, God's ancient promises to his people Israel. The reason why the new Covenant offers us what is called the Good News is thus evident. It is interesting to note, therefore, that the word *kaine* (new) does not occur in the more reliable manuscripts of Mark 14.24, Matt. 26.28, and Luke 22.20, which all describe the institution of the Lord's Supper, for the reason, as we have seen, that it was not necessary for it to be used at all; it might have created a false antithesis. 'The "New" Covenant is therefore *not* a *different* covenant, but the original Covenant established once and for all.'[1] 'Fundamentally the Old Testament teaches nothing other than what was taught by Christ.'[2]

We have now come to the point where we shall have to examine what it means when we speak of the New Testament as fulfilling the Old Testament before we can pursue our enquiry further.

---

[1] J. Jocz, *A Theology of Election*, 1958, p. 117.
[2] Th. C. Vriezen, *An Outline of Old Testament Theology*, 1958, p. 77.

8

'But I Say Unto You'

WHAT did our Lord himself have to say about the relationship between his words and the Law of Moses? We shall put together a few of his most important utterances on this point. It is understandable that St Matthew's Gospel has preserved most of these because of the latter's interest in what he believed to be the manner in which the Gospel of Christ fulfilled the Old Testament. But we also notice the interest of all four Evangelists in expounding this issue.

The question arises then, whether Jesus repudiated the Law of the Old Testament directly, when he pitted his '. . . but I say unto you' against the words, several times repeated in Matt. 5: 'Ye have heard that it was said by them of old time . . .' Now, the Pharisees of Jesus' day were the heritors of the Ezra tradition, and were legalistic in their turn of mind. They took the words of *Torah* literally and applied them to the very different situation of their own day. On the other hand, the translation 'Ye have heard' is not technical enough to be in accord with the Jewish usage of the period. At that time it meant, in discussions on the Law, 'Ye have understood literally.' This means that when Jesus used it he was saying: 'You might understand this command to mean literally "Thou shalt not kill", but I say . . .' and then goes on to give it a new depth and breadth that far surpasses the mere literal meaning.[1] More-

[1] David Daube, *The New Testament and Rabbinic Judaism*, 1956, pp. 55 ff.

over, Jews were on the whole accustomed to learning the content of Scripture from oral transmission, so I think we might also explain Jesus' phrase 'You have heard . . .' by expanding it to mean: 'You have heard in the reading of the Scripture in the synagogue services . . .'

In Matt. 5.21 our Lord quotes the Sixth Commandment. Then he adds: 'But I say unto you, That whosoever is angry with his brother . . .' This is evidently a reference to the oral interpretation of that commandment. But in v. 27 Jesus quotes the commandment about adultery, and at once adds his own interpretation: 'But I say unto you, that whosoever looketh on a woman to lust after her . . .' In v. 32 he adds to the law on divorce; in v. 34 to the law on swearing; in v. 39 to the *lex talionis* that we examined in chapter 3; in v. 44 to the law on loving and hating, and so on. In each case, we note, he *adds* to the Mosaic Law, expounding it, drawing it out to a new conclusion, personalizing it, 'interiorizing' it, so to speak. But not once does he abrogate the Mosaic Law on the basis of which he makes his new pronouncement.

What about the so-called 'food-laws' of the Mosaic Law? Did our Lord accept them, and expect his followers to be bound by them as well? In Matt. 15.10 ff. Jesus makes a direct reference to the food laws of both the Deuteronomic Code (Deut. 14.3-20) and the Priestly Code (Lev. 11). Once again we observe that he does not explicitly condemn them. (That he does so *implicitly*, however, is a point to which we shall return later.) What he does do is to add to the significance of those laws, using them as a means to a fuller appreciation of God's will for Israel. We have seen that Jeremiah looked for just such a 'fill-fullment' of the Mosaic Law. If Jesus had directly repudiated the food laws, then the hesitations of the primitive Church on this issue would be inexplicable (Acts 10.14; 15.28 f.; Rom. 14.14; Gal. 2.11-17;

Col. 2.20-22). What our Lord points out about the significance of the food laws, without repudiating them as such, is
well expressed by C. G. Montefiore: *'Things* cannot be
religiously either clean or unclean; only *persons*. And *persons* cannot be defiled by *things*, they can only be defiled by
themselves, by acting *irreligiously.'*[1]

Since, then, Christ never explicitly repudiates the Law,
whether it be an ethical commandment or a ceremonial, we
can now take the first step towards understanding his words
in the 'Sermon on the Mount' on this issue: 'Think not that
I am come to destroy the law, or the prophets: I am not
come to destroy, but to fulfil. For verily I say unto you, Till
heaven and earth pass, one jot or one tittle shall in no wise
pass from the law, till all be fulfilled. Whosoever therefore
shall break one of these least commandments, and shall
teach men so, he shall be called the least in the kingdom of
heaven: but whosoever shall do and teach them, the same
shall be called great in the kingdom of heaven' (Matt.
5.17-19).

In refusing to repudiate the Law of Moses Jesus is here in
full agreement with the passage in Jeremiah that we have
studied (Jer. 31.31 ff.). There we saw that Jeremiah never
supposed that God would set aside the Law which he had
given through Moses. To do so would make God unfaithful
to himself. Let us remind ourselves of the two emphases
which Jeremiah made, and to which we made reference in a
previous chapter: (1) when he says of God 'I will put my
law . . .' (v. 33) the law that Jeremiah speaks of is undoubtedly the Law of Moses, and not another and a new
law still to come. God will make a new *covenant* in days
to come, indeed; but as to a new law—no, such a thing
would be inconceivable. It would mean that the Psalmist
who wrote 'thy law is the truth' (Ps. 119.142) was not himself

[1] *The Synoptic Gospels*, vol. i, p. 153.

telling the truth. God had made a covenant already with Noah, that is to say, with the humanity that had escaped the outcome of God's righteous wrath upon human sin and apostasy (Gen. 9.8 ff.). He had made a special Covenant with Abraham, as the ancestor of one particular nation out of all the nations whom he had saved from the consequences of the Flood (Gen. 12.1-3; 15). And he had set his great Covenant upon the Israel that was actually descended from Abraham, this time at the foot of Mount Sinai (Ex. 19.3-6; 24.1-8). It should not therefore be a surprise to learn that Jeremiah expected God to make a new Covenant again with Israel, one that would mark the next and final step in the progression of covenants that he had already made. We say so because we have now learned that God is a God who likes covenants, and who obviously makes use of covenants to act as milestones in his advancing purpose for the redemption of the world.

(2) This leads us to refer back to the second emphasis in the promised new Covenant about which Jeremiah spoke. It was to be made *with Israel* (Jer. 31.33), and not with any other. Thus it is a gross misreading of Scripture to suppose that Jeremiah meant anything else than just what he said. The modern Gentile Christian can come close to heresy or even blasphemy in his arrogant reinterpretation of the Word of God. So often does he tacitly assume that Old Testament promises such as these cannot refer to the Jews, since 'the Jews killed Christ', but were spoken about the present-day Gentile Church to which he himself belongs. But we are always meant to sit humbly at the feet of the Scriptures, and ask ourselves what the Scriptures do actually say, and not expect them to say what we would like them to say. It is, then, a fact which Jeremiah definitely states: 'But this shall be the covenant that I will make with *the house of Israel* . . .' (Jer. 31.33). Yet we have already been alerted

to the fact that the prophetic understanding of the word 'Israel' does not necessarily mean the Hebrew people taken as a group and related by blood alone.

We are next to notice that our Lord himself was in full agreement with this promise that Jeremiah had uttered to Israel. In Matt. 10.5-6 Christ commands his disciples as follows: 'Go not into the way of the Gentiles, and into any city of the Samaritans enter ye not: but go rather to the lost sheep of the house of Israel.' (This last sentence is a direct reference to many Old Testament descriptions of Israel as sheep that are lost and need a shepherd, such as Ezek. 34; Jer. 23.1-4, etc.) Now, this command has given many Gentile Christians cause to pause and consider. But still more upsetting to the self-esteem of many Gentiles is our Lord's saying about his own mission, when confronted with a challenge to heal a Gentile child: 'I am not sent but unto the lost sheep of the house of Israel' (Matt. 15.24). St Paul confirms this statement in his great argument in Romans: 'For I tell you that Christ became a servant to the circumcised' (i.e. to the *Jews*) 'to show God's truthfulness (i.e. his reliability) in order to confirm the promises given to the patriarchs' (Rom. 15.8 RSV). St Paul has much more to say on this theme, but we shall return to his argument later. Yet we must be fully aware that for St Paul the Gospel (i.e. the content of *the new Covenant*) was to be preached 'to the Jew first' (i.e. to the people of *the old Covenant*): and that these words 'to the Jew first' he repeats on three occasions (Rom. 1.16; 2.9, 10). An examination of the background of our Lord's reply to the Syro-Phoenician woman (as we have the story in Matt. 15.21 ff.) may help us to see more clearly why both he and his disciple Paul make this, to us, seemingly extraordinary emphasis.

In our story we find the woman asking that her daughter should be healed. That was a small request. Any doctor,

even an unbelieving doctor, could attend to this sick child.
On the other hand, what was it that Christ gave to the sick
who came to him at Capernaum or Jerusalem, or anywhere
else *within the body of Israel with whom God had made his
Covenant and to whom God had given his Law*? He gave
them, not just healing for the body, he gave them *the Gospel*, the wholeness of which included far more than mere
healing for the body, and thus far more than the Syro-
Phoenician woman could ever understand. As a matter of
fact, many *Jews*, members of the old Covenant, did not
understand either just what Jesus had done for them. They
too thought that he had given them merely healing of the
body. That is why our Lord did not wish them to broadcast
a false and merely partial understanding of his messianic
function, and indeed told them not to do so. Merely to heal
the body of a Gentile child without offering the Gospel in
its fulness to that child's family and friends was a travesty
of what Christ had come into the world to do. It would in
fact be a casting of the bread of life to the unkempt dogs
that lived at the rubbish dumps, a casting of the pearl of the
Gospel before swine that could never, by the nature of
things, understand what they were in reality being offered.
Let us use the following picture. It would be a shame to
take infinite pains, over, shall we say, two thousand years
of God's activity within this world and in that period to
cook and bake a rich repast, and then to set a wide variety
of attractively prepared dishes of roast meats, spiced
viands, and elaborate sweets upon the table, that table
which was to be the Table of the Bridegroom's long-awaited
Supper with his friends whom God had summoned to the
feast from the days of Sinai, having prepared them over the
centuries for this great day of days—and then to open the
door and let in pigs to trample the feast in the mud as they
devoured it in their greed. Pigs need food if they are to live;

they need to be fed. If allowed in to the Feast the pigs
would get what they wanted—their bellies filled; the Syro-
Phoenician woman would get what she wanted—her
daughter cured. But neither could appreciate the significance of the Feast that was laid before them. Neither could
possibly receive what God had in mind to give them. His
loving purpose was simply incomprehensible to any woman
living outside of Israel, for the simple reason that it was
Israel alone that had been prepared to receive the fulness
of God's loving purpose—*and that was because Israel possessed the Law which God had given her through Moses at
Mount Sinai.* It is true that Christ heals this woman's
daughter. But he does so because he has found this woman
to be one of the few Gentiles aware that it was Israel alone
who was in the position to be invited to the Feast, with the
result that all she could expect to receive would be crumbs
that fell on the floor. She got her crumb. Her daughter was
healed. But in only a very restricted sense could she become
what in later years men began to call by the name of
Christian.

On the other hand, the God of the Bible is gracious beyond all human reckoning. There is no suggestion here that,
despite her deficiencies of understanding, this woman was
excluded from the Kingdom. She was surely one of those
of whom Christ said: 'And I say unto you, That many shall
come from the east and west, and shall sit down with Abraham, and Isaac, and Jacob, in the kingdom of heaven'
(Matt. 8.11). 'God is not bound by his Sacraments' declared
the Reformers four centuries ago. 'Nor by his chosen mode
of working through Covenant relationships' we might add
at this point in our discussion. The Syro-Phoenician woman
is like the workman hired at the eleventh hour, but who
receives the full pay at the end of the day (Matt. 20.1-16), as
are serious-minded Confucianists and Moslems, and Hindus

and modern agnostics. It is a confusion of ideas to suppose that because the latter are excluded from the Covenant they are therefore excluded from the Kingdom.

What is there in Israel in which the Syro-Phoenician woman could not share? What marked off Israel from all the Gentile peoples of the earth? What was the essential nature of Israel's heritage that made her, and her alone, the seed-bed in which the Gospel could grow and expand? St Paul has a ready answer: 'They are Israelites, and to them belong the sonship, the glory, the covenants, the giving of the law, the worship, and the promises; to them belong the patriarchs, and of their race, according to the flesh, is the Christ' (Rom. 9.4-5 RSV).

'To them belong the sonship.' We are to remember that when God called Israel out of Egypt, he explicitly declared that the whole people of Israel was his firstborn son (Ex. 4.22). The firstborn was naturally the most beloved of all the children, and so it is also natural that the word 'first-born' could be used synonymously with 'beloved'. Israel was God's beloved son. A son for twelve hundred years now! Surely the *content* of his life must be very different from that of the orphan who has to beg for a living at the gates of an eastern city! 'What advantage then hath the Jew?' Gentiles asked St Paul (Rom. 3.1). What a silly thing to say! But then what orphan, *while he is still an orphan*, can ever know the blessedness of being a son? It would be like asking a boy of fifteen to write an essay on what it means to be in love. 'To them belongs the glory'—the glory that was the self-manifestation of the living God made comprehensible to the eyes and hearts of his creature man under guise of a pillar of cloud by day and a pillar of fire by night (Ex. 13.21-22). 'In the morning, then ye shall see the glory of the Lord,' said Moses and Aaron to Israel (Ex. 16.7) . . . 'and behold the glory of the Lord appeared in the cloud' (Ex. 16.10). 'And the glory of the Lord abode upon Mount Sinai' (Ex. 24.16). What did the Syro-Phoenician woman know of any of this self-manifestation of the God who had created the heavens and the earth when he 're-vealed' his mind and purpose to Israel in the days of Moses?

'To them belong the covenants.' The Gentiles knew nothing of the joy of having been chosen in order to serve, and in serving to come to know the fellowship of the living God. (See Ps. 105.6-8; Isa. 42.1; 43.20; 65.9.)

'The giving of the Law.' So there it is. The *Torah* is God's gift to Israel, and to Israel alone. 'What advantage then hath the Jew? or what profit is there in circumcision?' 'Much every way,' Paul replies to his questioner. 'Chiefly because that unto them were committed the oracles of God' —another word for the *Torah* (Rom. 3.1-2). And with the oracles went 'the service of God', both at the Tabernacle and Temple, and in the ordinary tasks of life;[1] 'and the promises', made to Abraham, Isaac and Jacob, and renewed in the promise of a new Covenant in Jeremiah 31. 'Whose are the fathers' refers to the Patriarchs, who had answered God's first call in faith, especially Abraham, whom the Creator of the ends of the earth was not ashamed to call his friend (Isa. 41.8).

All this, then, was the seed-bed of the message of Christ. The Gospel of Christ could take on its fulness and express itself in its wholeness *only* as the filling-full of those things which were of advantage to the Jew. The Syro-Phoenician woman could not conceivably understand this, although, as we have seen, she had a sufficient glimmer of it for our Lord to use for her eventual advantage. It is no surprise to us that

[1] How deep this idea of service penetrated into primitive Christianity is shown by such passages as I Cor. 9.19; II Cor. 4.5; Gal. 5.13. The Pope's title became *servus servorum Dei*, 'servant of the servants of God'.

the disciples for all their obtuseness about the mission of
Christ certainly realized that this woman was not in the
position to appreciate what Christ had come into the world
to do. Nor is it a surprise to read that the moment Jesus
returned to the area where the 'Covenant People' dwelt,
what happened was that '. . . great multitudes came unto
him, having with them those that were lame, blind, dumb,
maimed, and many others . . . and he healed *them* . . .
and they glorified the God of *Israel'* (Matt. 15.30-31).

Our examination of the above incident has begun to show
us what the Gospel really involves, our subject of enquiry
in chapter 2. Clearly it is not a message merely summoning
isolated individual souls to faith. While it is necessarily addressed to individuals, these must respond to its call to
enter into the mighty heritage that God has already given
to the Jews, the heritage which St Paul describes to his
Roman readers. On the other hand, this heritage of the old
Covenant is not to be identified with the Kingdom of God,
and those who belong within it are not to be thought of as
already 'saved' when others are not. Rather, God elected his
Covenant People in order that they should be his witnesses
and servant in the world (Isa. 43.10). It is surely important
then for God that his witnesses should be thoroughly
trained and should find their roots deep down in his abiding
purpose for mankind.

Now, the culmination of St Paul's argument in our passage in Romans is that our Lord himself is rooted in this
heritage of Israel. So we must now seek to determine what
difference it makes for us today that St Paul can conclude
the list of the Jew's advantages by declaring: '. . . of whom,
as concerning the flesh, Christ came.'

9

Christ, the End of the Law—I

'OF whom, as concerning the flesh, Christ came.' In the previous chapter we saw how St Paul regarded Christ as the *end* of the purpose which God had had in mind when he called Israel to be his instrument for the salvation of the world (Rom. 9.4-5). Christ is the ultimate *end* of all the promises made to the patriarchs, and so to Israel through the mouths of the prophets. He is thus the ultimate end of *Israel* itself, because he is the outcome of all the heritage that Israel alone possessed. If it could be said of Israel 'he is my son' (Ex. 4.22), then how much more could it not also be said of Christ? Had not the glory rested upon *him* as well, upon the mount of Transfiguration (Mark 9.2 =Matt. 17.1 ff.=Luke 9.28 ff.), the very glory that Israel had witnessed upon the mount up which Moses had gone to talk with God? If the Law had taught men to worship God at the sanctuary, then how much more had not Christ taught men so to do? Was Christ himself not the great High Priest whose mediation was that of both God and man at once? (Heb. 4.14-16). Had he not brought men to God by actually becoming the sanctuary himself, to the extent that, should the sanctuary in Jerusalem be overthrown, his body, which was in reality the temple of God on earth, would be raised again on the third day? (John 2.19-21). Was it not the purpose of the Law, moreover, to reveal the very mind of God to Israel; yet who did just that if it was not Christ? Yet what does it mean when we say that Christ is the *end* of the

Law? Obviously we shall have to look more closely now at this word *end*.

In the first place, we should recall that our Lord nowhere repudiates the Law. We saw that while he *deduced* the Law, and so 'interiorized' it, and gave it new content and depth, yet he never abrogated it in his teaching. All that 'Moses' had to say, he believed, came to its final 'end' in what *he* had to say, as he taught men by showing the continuity between Moses and himself in the words 'Ye have heard that it was said by them of old time . . . but I say unto you . . .'

Then in the second place we are to note that Christ believed that he not only taught the fulness of the Law, but that he himself also *kept* the whole Law. We have said that he repudiated neither the moral nor the ceremonial Law. That means that when he exclaimed 'Which of you convinceth me of sin?' (John 8.46), a Johannine question which evidently reflects the impression he left upon his disciples, he included within that challenge reference to the transgression of *all* elements constitutive of the Law of Moses. That is to say, Jesus believed himself to be the only Israelite, the only member of the Covenant People, ever to have been able to keep the Law to perfection. The Law thus found itself incarnate for the first time. The Law, which Ps. 119 had called 'the Truth, the Word of God', had thus now become flesh at last. Jesus of Nazareth was thus, as he himself believed, the *end* of the Law.

Now, this word 'end' is not used in the New Testament as we would use it when we speak merely of the last in a series. A railway train has twelve carriages, let us say; therefore one of those carriages must be the 'end' carriage. Rather, St Paul's use of *telos*, 'end', as applied to Christ, where he says that Christ is 'the end of the Law' (Rom. 10.4), just as St Peter says he is the 'end' of our faith (I Peter 1.9), is a carrying over into the Greek language of an Old Testament idea contained in the Hebrew word *'aharith*. The content of this word will therefore occupy us for the next few pages. This word *'aharith* is usually translated by the English word 'end'. But we shall hope to show that it is rather the 'out-come' of a particular course of action that the Hebrew word is seeking to express, so that our word 'meaning' may perhaps translate it better than the word 'end'.

The Hebrews were utterly convinced of the unitary nature of this world that God had made. Nowhere in the Old Testament do we find the idea many hold today that perhaps there are really two worlds after all—the world of things, that we can see and handle and manipulate, and the world of spirit, invisible to our eyes. To speak of 'the world beyond' as if it were the 'real' world, is therefore *wrong*, from the standpoint of the Old Testament. Which shows how many people today, even believing people, are far from understanding the basis of their faith—and how quite un-wittingly they depend upon the philosophy of the Greeks rather than upon the Word of God for an understanding of the world they live in! An instance of this is the prevailing belief amongst Christians in the immortality of the soul. Many believers despair of this world, they despair of any meaning in a world where suffering and frustration seem to rule. And so they look for a release for their souls from the weight of the flesh, and they hope for an entry into 'the world of the spirit', as they call it, a place where their souls will find a blessedness they cannot discover in the flesh. A suicide leaves a note to say that he is going to join his beloved in 'the other world', as if there could be 'another world' that he could enter unconnected with his state of mind and his re-lationship to God here and now. The Old Testament, which was of course the Scriptures of the early Church, has no word at all for the modern (or ancient Greek) idea of 'soul'.

We have no right to read this modern word into St Paul's Greek word *psyche*; for by it he was not expressing what Plato had meant by the word, he was expressing what Isaiah and what Jesus meant by it.

In the Old Testament man is never considered to be a soul dwelling in a body, a soul that will one day be set free from the oppression of the body, at the death of that body, like a bird released from a cage. The Hebrews were not dualists in their understanding of God's world. They believed that just as there is one God, and one alone, so there is only one world, and one alone, not a world of the spirit *and* a world of matter. Thus they also believed that man, being part of the world, is necessarily but one also. That is not to say that the Hebrews were 'materialists', to use a modern term, and that they believed in nothing beyond what they could see and touch. On the contrary, they were emphatic in their belief that God had made both heaven *and* earth. Once again, however, such a phrase does not imply a dualism of thought. The reason is that heaven was just as material a place to the Hebrews as was the earth! It too was created, although invisible to our eyes. Heaven was, in fact, one in essence with the earth beneath. That is why God does not dwell in heaven. God dwells *above* the heavens. 'Behold, the heaven, and heaven of heavens cannot contain thee' (I Kings 8.27), said Solomon at the dedication of the Temple. Or again, the angels are at times equated with the stars. This is because *nothing* in heaven or earth can be compared with God himself, who is the creator of *all things* —creator of *both heaven and earth.*

This is not the place to continue the discussion of what the Bible teaches about the 'soul' and about what happens to it after death. But there is one thing sure we can say at this point and that is that the popular doctrine of the soul's immortality cannot be traced back to a biblical teaching. It is Animists, Spiritualists, Mohammedans, and men and women of many other faiths who hold to some form of a conception of the immortality of the soul; far less then is it originally a Christian doctrine. This is because the doctrine is essentially man-centred, selfish and materialistic. What the Bible does offer us is *Christ*, the living Christ, the resurrected Christ, the life-giving because he is the forgiving Christ. 'To me to live is Christ,' exclaims St Paul (Phil. 1.21); therefore 'to die is gain'. St Paul knew that there was nothing in himself that was inherently worthy of surviving death. But if, on the contrary, he were 'in Christ', as he knew himself to be, then nothing in heaven or earth, including death itself, could separate him from the risen and living Christ, who had broken down by his atoning life and death the wall of separation that had blocked for man the way to God.

The Old Testament writers are well aware that beyond the reach of the senses and of human knowledge there is a realm of the mysterious, or the numinous, in and through which God manifests himself to men just as much as he does through matter and the senses of the body. But to recognize this fact in no way militates against the conviction of all writers in the Old Testament, with the possible exception of the book of Ecclesiastes, that this universe is one and indivisible.

Beginning from this basis, then, the writers of the Old Testament accepted as axiomatic that there must be a vital union between the unknown world and that in which we live. And since this world is *real*, and life as it has to be lived on this planet also is *real*, then the world of the unseen must be as real as the world we live in. The poet Longfellow's questioner would have been quite out of place in Isaiah's company. Isaiah would have been shocked to hear him declare that this life is 'but an empty dream'.[1] No, says the Old Testament, with emphasis, this life is real, because God has made it, and has made it well.

Has the Old Testament then nothing to say about a life beyond? It is true that in only a few late passages is specific mention made of a life beyond (cf. Isa. 25.8; 26.19; Dan. 12.2), apart from the primitive notion of *Sheol*, the abode of the dead, that Israel shared with most of her neighbours for many hundreds of years. But faith had been reaching out to belief in a life after death long before those passages were penned, as we can see from the utterances of more than one Psalmist and other writers (cf. Ps. 16.9-10; 49.15; 73.25-26; Job 14.13-15; 19.25-27). On the other hand, faith made this outreach simply because the great souls throughout Old Testament times were wholly convinced that life lived here upon this earth was the gift of God, and was thus necessarily *meaningful* and relevant, not just for *here and now*, but also in relation to the *whole* cosmos of God's creation, i.e. to both 'earth' and 'heaven'.

As a corollary to this view of God's creation, the Hebrews maintained still another emphasis upon the relationship between 'the two worlds', closely related as they are to each other like the two sides to a coin. Life on this earth is a growing and developing life, and not a static one. This must mean that it is the invisible world which is affected by the life men live upon this earth, and not primarily the other way round. It is this life that is basic for the life of the world to come. That is why there is no faintest suggestion in the Old Testament of the idea in any form of the pre-existence of the soul. The Old Testament writers knew that it is in this world of space and time that the human ego has been given the opportunity to grow and develop. This meant that this world is *real* to a degree that no other faith has ever maintained, and it means too that life lived here and

---

[1] H. W. Longfellow, *A Psalm of Life*.

now is life lived in total earnest. That is why we can say with very great emphasis that this life has meaning.

'The Lord *is* my salvation,' exclaims the Psalmist, 'here and now' (Ps. 62.2; 118.14; Isa. 12.2); and he certainly means that since the Lord is himself eternal, his own salvation now contains within it validity for the world to come. '*Today*, if ye will hear his voice, harden not your heart,' declares another (Ps. 95.7-8). In light of such a faith, the Psalmist might well have replied to the man who hoped to 'meet' his beloved 'over there': '*Today* does not mean *in the future*, in the life to come; for you create your future *now* by the manner in which you handle every moment that you have.' 'Prepare to meet your God,' *now*, exclaims the prophet Amos (Amos 4.12), not in the realm of the dead, *after* this life is over, but in the shops and stalls in the streets of Bethel; for *now* is in vital unity with the whole of reality, and so is in complete unity with the world to come.

This refusal by the writers of the Old Testament to separate the realm of the 'spiritual' from the realm of the 'material' results in making Israel's thought a seemingly very earthy thing. But it is earthy only in so far that it derives from the faith that when God made *this* world he saw that it was good. Since God has made it as it is, then everything that is good must be of eternal significance; it must have an *'aharith*—an ultimate outcome, an *end*. The outcome of 'Jacob's' sin, says Micah poetically (1.4-5) will be the melting of the mountains. Incidentally that is why the Old Testament (and the New!) looks forward to an *end* of the world which will not necessarily be the last event to take place in history, the end carriage of a long, long railway train, but will be the total *'aharith*, the ultimate expression of the meaning, not just of this world, but of all God's creation, visible and invisible. 'For behold, I create new heavens and a new earth, and the former shall not be remembered, nor come into mind' (Isa. 65.17; cf. 66.22; Rev. 21.1). Here we see that both heaven and earth are to be re-newed, because, as we have realized, ultimately speaking, the two are one. Consequently both are to find their *'aḥarith* together, when God's good time arrives.

St Paul now claims that this *end* of the world has come; in fact, he dogmatically states that the *ends* of both of the two worlds have arrived (*ta tele ton aionon*, I Cor. 10.11). This is language like that used by British Railways, where owing to the exigencies of the English language a plural must be employed in notices on trains: 'Passengers are warned not to put their heads out of the carriage window.' Yet Paul can also speak of the 'end' of the old world as the beginning of a new creation wherein all things are made new (II Cor. 5.17). He does so because logical thought de-mands that we should finally come to the last carriage of our railway train, that is to say, that we must finally reach the last day in chronological time, and so come to 'the end of the world'. The Old Testament does, of course, mark the passage of clock time by means of hours, days and years. Yet its concern is not so much with what we would regard as a scientific concept of time as with time as God-given opportunity to obey and do God's will.[1] The New Testa-ment continues to use this 'theological', rather than 'scien-tific', view of the word. That is why it can concern itself vitally with the possibility of the 'end of the world' happen-ing in the life-time of the first generation of the new Church, so that Paul can suppose clock time as already pointing to five minutes to twelve. Yet, just as for the Chris-tian real death happens at the moment of his baptism (Rom. 6.4), with the result that when for him the clock strikes twelve and he meets what we mortals know of as physical

---

[1] See article 'Time' by John Marsh, in *A Theological Wordbook of the Bible*, 1950.

death, that moment now loses its original significance, so too in the case of the end of history. Time for St Paul has already met with its 'end' in the death and resurrection of Christ, so that the last day of the world is a date which has no more significance than any other day in the world's calendar. On the other hand, Christ, as the end of all things, and thus the beginning of the new, is by the same token also the end of the Law of the Old Testament and so is the beginning of something which now fulfils the old Law, and makes the Law the touchstone for a new, full, and comprehensive relationship between God and his Covenant People.

FOR FURTHER READING

W. D. Davies, *Paul and Rabbinic Judaism*, 1948.
W. D. Davies, *Torah in the Messianic Age and/or the World to Come*, 1952.
James Parkes, *Jesus, Paul and the Jews*, 1936.

10

Christ, the End of the Law—II

BEFORE we look to see what the above conclusion means for the relationship between Law and Gospel, there is another aspect of the significance of the *Torah* which will now be very obvious to us, and that is the simple proposition that the legal element in what we call the Law of Moses has to do with matters touching not only this life here and now, but also the world to come. Yet at once this whole conception seems to be at variance with what we have already seen the Law to be. We have already seen that in large part the Law has to do with the regulating of human relationships within the community of Israel. We have seen that it has much to say on economics, on family life, on rules for war, on hygiene, on behaviour within the various groupings of human society, and so on. That is to say, the Law is not at all an 'otherworldly' code. It does not ostensibly concern itself with the preparation of the soul for the beyond. Of course it has much to say on the regulation of worship. But the worship for which it legislates is not directed to 'the world to come'. It is directed to the world of 'here and now'. It sees worship as the solvent of human ills in this world of space and time. It offers a cult which will explain to the worshipper what God is doing at the present moment within his present society, and in the setting of his own home and family life. It is not its primary intention to provide the Israelite with a means of 'deepening his spiritual life' in a pietistic sense. What it does do is to offer him the opportunity and the strength to obey the voice of God in his ordinary daily life *here and now*. But now the relevance of what we have been emphasizing in the previous chapter will have become plain to us at this point. It is just because the Law is so wholly relevant to the establishment of the good life *here and now*, that it is at the same time also essentially relevant for the establishment of the good life *there and then*. The Law, in reality, actually teaches the significant truth that in being obedient to the voice of God here and now, the ordinary Israelite is building for himself a relationship to God that must have ultimate significance for, and that must be eternally valid in, 'the heavenly places'.

At this point we may reiterate that the Old Testament, with its unitary view of life, draws no line between what we today differentiate as moral and ceremonial laws. The ceremonial laws, and the laws regulating the cult as practised at the Temple, contribute to the upbuilding of Israel's society as a community of *persons* under God just as much as do the moral laws that we call the Decalogue. Since such is the case, it means that Christ fulfilled both the moral law and the ceremonial law.

The greater part of the Psalter came to be used in Israel's worship to supplement and expound the cultic acts of the priests when they were serving at the altar. Now, it is in large part from the Psalter that we can see how the ultimate significance of what Israel was doing in her acts of worship in obedience to the Law's demands was, under God, becoming evident to thoughtful minds. The meaningfulness of the *Torah* in this life, Israel had begun to see, necessarily involved its meaningfulness for all eternity. If the *Torah* taught man to worship God here and now in fellowship with his brethren, then that worship must have meaning in the beyond. And that meaning could only be a living fellowship with the living God in the world to come. But an understanding of that meaningfulness was contributed to by the ceremonial law just as much as by the Ten Commandments. A good example of this latter truth is evidenced by the use that Israel made of Psalm 51. This most deeply 'spiritual' of Psalms, in which the singer, more than anywhere else in the Old Testament, seeks longingly for the forgiveness of God: 'Create in me a clean heart, O God; and renew a right spirit within me' (v. 10), ends with a verse that comes as an unpleasant surprise: 'Then shalt thou be pleased with the sacrifices of righteousness, with burnt offering and whole burnt offering: then shall they offer bullocks upon thine altar.' Yet, of course, it is only the modern reader who is surprised at the inclusion of this verse. Post-exilic Judaism recognized that the offering of bullocks upon God's altar was a sacramental sign and seal of God's forgiveness of the offerer's sin, and was therefore as fully significant for the upholding of the Covenant as the keeping of the Ten Commandments could ever be. *Everything*, then, with which the Law was concerned, both moral and ceremonial, bore for the believing Israelite an ultimate *end* and significance.

Now, as we have said, the Law of Moses concerns itself greatly with ways and means for Israel to live together in society as a human fellowship. That is to say, the *Torah* aims at producing a state of *shalom* in Israelite society. This is the word we usually translate as 'peace'. In the modern State of Israel, the word is the regular good wish used by Jew to Jew, and means 'good morning', 'good evening', or 'goodbye', as the case may be. But as a result of the prophetic interpretation of God's will for Israel *shalom* had come to mean that perfect harmony between man and man that comes about when individuals have learned to love and respect one another, under God. The idea of *shalom* there-

fore covered the application of those laws on economic matters which we have looked at, and of all the other laws that
regulate the life of man as *communal* man in the daily
existence of the Covenant People. The 'peace' that the Old
Testament looks forward to in the future therefore is one
where (as Micah sums it up) men will act with justice to each
other, will love the covenant relationship which God has
created as the basis of all meaningfulness in life, and where
men and women will each, as individuals, walk humbly with
their God (Micah 6.8). That is to say, the Law sought to
establish within the earthly city of Jerusalem a perfect community life. The sinful inhabitants of that city, it is true,
were never able to 'keep the Law' in that respect, nor intro-
duce that true *shalom* or 'peace' within the city which
Isaiah had envisaged would one day come to pass when 'the
mountain of the Lord's house shall be established in the
top of the mountains, and shall be exalted above the hills;
and all nations shall flow unto it. And many people shall go
and say, Come ye, and let us go up to the mountain of the
Lord, to the house of the God of Jacob; and he will teach
us of his ways, and we will walk in his paths: for out of
Zion shall go forth the law, and the word of the Lord from
Jerusalem. And he shall judge among the nations, and shall
rebuke many people: and they shall beat their swords into
plowshares, and their spears into pruninghooks: nation
shall not lift up sword against nation, neither shall they
learn war any more' (Isa. 2.2-4). Yet it was the great hope of
Israel's prophets that that day would certainly dawn. That
would be the day when the Law, which offered Israel a
vision of true peace, would meet its *end*.

The Church believes, with Paul, that the *end* of the Law
did come. It believes that it came with him who said:
'*Shalom* I leave with you, my *shalom* I give unto you: not
as the world giveth give I unto you' (John 14.27); but rather

as 'Moses' had already prescribed long ago in the Law, and as Jeremiah had expected, that *shalom* would once and for all become incarnate for men.

The *shalom* that Christ has offered us, then, is a whole, new, perfect and complete way of life, made known to us in our personal experience and in our communal life alike, made known to us *here and now* within the Covenant People that is his Church, yet valid through its essential reality for the whole of God's great creation, and so also for the world to come. The framework or scaffolding of that *shalom* God has given to us through the hand of Moses in the Law. The *end* of that *shalom*, however, God has given to us in the person of his only Son our Lord.

FOR FURTHER READING

H. Wheeler Robinson, *Inspiration and Revelation in the Old Testament*, 1946.
John Marsh, *The Fulness of Time*, 1952.
O. Cullmann, *Christ and Time*, 1950.
Floyd V. Filson, *The Gospel according to St. Matthew*, 1960.
C. H. Dodd, *The Epistle of Paul to the Romans*, 1932.
Karl Barth, *A Shorter Commentary on Romans*, 1959.
T. W. Manson, *Ethics and the Gospel*, 1960.
Karl Barth, *God, Grace and Gospel*, 1959.
C. H. Dodd, *Gospel and Law*, 1951.
T. W. Manson, *The Teaching of Jesus*, 1931.

Grafting into the Olive

THE reader will have noticed that up to this point we
have refrained from assigning any significance to the
Law with reference to ourselves as modern Christians.
And yet the whole purpose of this book is to examine what
the Law has to say to us, and to discover whether we who
are Gentile Christians ought to keep the Law of Moses in
any sense at all. We have refrained from doing so, of course,
because of the explicit teaching of the New Testament itself
in the matter. The New Testament does not declare that
Christ is the *end* of the Law for *us*; but it does declare that
Christ is the *end* of the Law for Israel. Let us look once
again at Paul's important argument in Rom. 9.3b-5: '. . . my
brethren, my kinsmen according to the flesh: who are
Israelites; to whom pertaineth the adoption, and the glory,
and the covenants, and the giving of the law, and the service of God, and the promises; whose are the fathers, and of
whom, as concerning the flesh, Christ came.' We Gentile
Christians should note, however, that we do not by nature
possess this adoption spoken of here. That is, it is not *our*
ancestors to whom God said, 'You, Israel, are my son' (Ex.
4.22). It was not to *our* ancestors that the Glory was revealed. Ours were then roaming in the gloom of the forests
of the Rhine or on the steppes of Siberia. God made no
covenant with the Saxons or the Picts or the Normans, nor
did he ever reveal himself to our ancestors through a *Torah*
meant for us. That is not to deny that our pagan ancestors

had some conception of right and wrong (Rom. 2.14-15). Yet it was not we who were called to the service of God, nor were our ancestors given any promises by God in any form. We were aliens and orphans, like the Syro-Phoenician woman, or any other non-Israelite of any nationality. Our ancestors combined in human societies that could have had no conception of what Micah was talking about in 700 BC when he declared that the application of the *Torah* to human life would bring about the rule of social justice. How could the ancient Britons have glimpsed the idea, integral to the whole Old Testament, of loyalty to a revealed way of life? In consequence, and to refer again to Micah 6.8, the individual in our Gentile societies in days of old was naturally quite unaware of the possibility of being able to walk humbly with his God.

The answer to this seeming *contretemps* that faces the Gentile who desires to become a believer in Christ is of course given us in the New Testament. It is the answer which Paul has shown in Galatians and in Romans as the only possible means of meeting this problem. The Gentile, whether he be the Syro-Phoenician woman, the medieval Englishman, or the modern citizen of New York, cannot conceivably know the fulness of life that is in Christ unless (and here we use St Paul's vivid metaphor) he is first *grafted into Israel*. What then did Paul mean by such a phrase? (Rom. 11.17 ff.). We have to turn to the science of horticulture to find the answer.

The art of the horticulturist has placed many lovely and varied roses in our modern gardens. But none of these beautiful cultured flowers, we all know if we are gardeners, has a root that was originally its own. In each and every case the cultured rose has had to be grafted on to the root of a wild brier. There may be a hundred varieties of roses, some giving pink, some giving yellow or mauve flowers, some producing a multitude of heads, some rambling or climbing over trellises or walls, but each and all have originally been grafted on to a wild root, the root of the wild rose that grows as a pest in the woods. St Paul, as we know, employed this horticultural analogy in order to make plain in his teaching how the Gentile believer, if he is to know the fulness of the biblical faith that is now contained in both Testaments, must first be grafted or inserted into the root that is none other than the ancient People of God, that people whom God had trained and disciplined for himself for nearly two thousand years. Yet Paul, city dweller though he is, now does a remarkable thing with his analogy; in fact, he tampers with nature, so to speak. But he does so deliberately, with the end in view of shaking us Gentile Christians into awareness that the vitally important thing which has happened to us is something that is quite contrary to the ways of nature. The picture that he draws of the grafting process is naturally not that of the modern rose. He chooses the olive tree that every Mediterranean inhabitant recognized at sight (Rom. 11.13-24). But now, in his parable, Paul proceeds to do the impossible thing. He speaks of grafting *wild* olive shoots into a *cultivated* olive tree, the wild shoots now taking the place of some natural branches that had ceased to bear fruit as they ought. What he meant, of course, was that the People of God, Israel, is the cultivated tree (see, e.g., Jer. 11.16), cultivated as it had been now by God for two thousand years before the coming of Christ; and that it was the Gentile Church which was the wild and uncultured plant, or uncultured shoots. This was because it was the Gentile Church which did not possess 'the adoption, and the glory, and the covenants . . .' and all the rest. And so Paul comes to the amazing yet heartening conclusion that God in his infinite mercy and goodness has willed to graft us uncultivated Gentiles into the great heritage of the people of the old Covenant made at Sinai.

What varieties of believers in Christ there are today—white men, black men, pygmies, intellectuals, labourers! But the inference that we receive from St Paul's teaching is that every single Gentile Christian on this earth, whatever the marks of his diversity may be, must necessarily be grafted into the stock and root of Israel if he is ever to know what it really means to be 'in Christ'. The very idea of having to be grafted into Israel, however, strikes many Gentile Christians as being in the nature of a 'scandal'. The Hitler in us all, that believes there is something inherently good within our own ego that God can use to his glory, rebels at having to stoop to receive into our blood-stream the life-giving flow of the sap that rises from Jewish roots, from Mosaic patterns of thought, from Hebraic and not Socratic (and thus Aryan-European!) discoveries of the ways of God with man. And so men refuse to face the challenge of Christ and prefer to turn their back upon the clear thinking of St Paul. The result is that their Christianity is often an emasculated Christianity. We can observe their individualistic conception of the Faith; it is often an interpretation of the New Testament which they believe accords well with the rugged individualism of what they understand to be the democracy of the twentieth century. This heresy has bedevilled the Church's life not only at the present day, but all down the centuries in various forms. Within a hundred years of the preaching of Peter and Paul a theologian by the name of Marcion (*c*. AD 140) was declared to be a heretic for holding views similar to the above. He rejected the Old Testament as the Word of God for Gentile Christians. But we do not need to range over the last two thousand years to follow out this heresy in its many manifestations. We need only look around us today.

Although this is a democratic era, paradoxically enough, modern man is less of an individualist than was his grandfather a century ago. Modern factory man, indeed, can scarcely make up his own mind as an individual on any topic of consequence. The group makes it up for him instead. The mass of people in most present-day countries with no more to their credit than a primary education, similarly depends for a lead to their thinking upon the mass media of propaganda—the Sunday paper, TV, and so on. In fact, the masses are content simply to be part of a great social system which controls, guides and sways nine-tenths of their thoughts and actions. A century ago the individualistic presentation of the Gospel, what we have come to look back on as the Victorian presentation of it, received a hearing by far greater numbers of the population than it is ever likely to do today. That presentation of the Gospel was frequently one which challenged the individual only to give himself in faith to Christ. The result was that a 'single-channeled' Gospel such as it often was cut deep into a person's life. The Victorian era was the age of great individualists, of convictions deeply held; it was the great age of the expansion of individualistic Protestant missions, of the growth of the Bible Societies, Sunday schools and so on; and today many good church people look back with nostalgia upon those great days of packed churches and liberal donations for Christian missions.

But the reason for the wide response to preaching a century ago was the fact that, by and large, the Gospel was usually presented on a narrow (and therefore, often, a really deep) basis to the individual, *as* an individual. And a century ago the individual was individual enough to make a response. Today, however, the same individualistic call to repent and believe is presented to men and women who are not individuals any longer, and so, again by and large, who do not understand the call, and cannot make the response the preacher expects. It may well be that, within the providence of God, modern mass man will really understand and respond to the challenge of the Gospel only on that day when we shall have learned how to present it as St Paul meant it to be presented. The *whole* Gospel must comprise the combination of the offer of forgiveness and new life to the individual that Christ has brought, with that new life rooted in another offer, that of the redeemed society for which Moses legislated but which has also found its *end* in Christ.

On the other hand, we would do well to recall that when the early Church summarized the Gospel call in the words we have used above, viz., 'Repent, and believe,' or 'Believe on the Lord Jesus Christ and thou shalt be saved,' it too was addressing the Gospel to men and women who were certainly not individualists either in the Victorian or in the modern sense of the word. This is because those to whom the call was addressed were Jews! When, for example, the rich young ruler came running to our Lord with the eager question: 'Master, what shall I do that I may inherit eternal life?' what was Jesus' reply? It was no less than 'Thou knowest the commandments' (Mark 10:19). Eternal life was rooted in the Law of Moses. But then, as we have said, a Jewish youth would naturally think in terms of the Law of Moses. What about the Ethiopian eunuch whom Philip baptized right at the beginning of the Church's story? (Acts 8.26-40). There we read how Philip baptized a Gentile, a foreigner, a black man, a eunuch; and be it noted that eunuchs ought not to share in the heritage of Israel according to the Law (Deut. 23.1; Isa. 56.3). Why is it then that in this story Philip, without hesitation, proceeds to baptize this total outcast into Christ, the King and Head of the Church, when Christ himself had referred the rich young ruler first of all back to the Law, and in the case of the Syro-Phoenician woman had obviously not found it possible to do for her what Philip was now doing for the eunuch?

In the case of the rich young ruler Jesus is able to begin by reminding him of his unique and God-given heritage. This young Jew already possessed the blue-print, so to speak, of the new society for which Christ would have men live. But he still needed a change of heart, as an individual, if he was ever to know what a wonderful heritage he possessed. Now, it was just this wonderful heritage of the *Jew* that the Ethiopian eunuch had obviously begun to appreciate. We remember that he had been fascinated by the 53rd chapter of Isaiah, the portrait of the Suffering Servant. And while we are given only a short vignette, only a few verses long, as is the case with so many of the stories in the New Testament, it is obvious that the eunuch had been realizing that in some manner that challenged his whole soul and mind, this unknown Servant was the key to the whole Pentateuch which he must have been reading as well. In other words, the eunuch was more truly a Jew in spirit than was the rich young ruler, and in the sense that Paul was later to use, he had been already grafted through the power of God's Spirit, by faith, into the heritage that God had given to Israel of old. That is why Philip is able to baptize him at once, because he knows that the Ethiopian can now comprehend the full significance of what it means to be grafted into the Law as it has now found its *end* in Christ.

Or again, let us take the story of St Peter and the sheet let down from heaven as we find it in Acts 10.11. From all that we are able to learn of Peter in the Gospels and in the Epistles, he was slower in recognizing that Jesus was the *end* of the Law than Philip had been. He had not been able to reconcile, for example, the items in the 'Holiness Code' or the command not to eat certain meats, as listed in Deut. 14.3 ff., with the fulfilment of the Law in Christ. Poor Peter needs to be given a special revelation, a dream all for himself (Acts 10) before he can grasp what it means that Christ is indeed the *end* of the Law. But once he has received that revelation Peter is utterly convinced of its truth and relevance and is now in full agreement with St Paul as to what the 'wholeness' of the Gospel must mean. The whole Gospel must be no less that the new life, with its full and free forgiveness, and hope for beyond the grave which Christ has come to offer. But the power of his Spirit has released that life in the hearts of individuals to the full only when they are set within that all-embracing communal fellowship which we call the Church. It is the Church, therefore, which is now the fulfilment of the ideal of *shalom* for which Moses legislated and of which he spoke. That then is how the Gentiles who are grafted into the Church from out of every race and nation of men under the sun are actually at the same time grafted into the Israel with whom God entered into covenant in the first place.

4

12

'One Jot or One Tittle'

THE question must now be asked—did our Lord in fact really keep the Law of Moses? For the Pharisees do not seem to have thought that he did. We have seen that he himself accepted the Decalogue as from the hand of Moses, obeying it consequently as coming from God (see Mark 7.10; 10.3, etc.). But he seems to have harboured an attitude to the Law which the Pharisees at least declared was sufficient to condemn him as a lawbreaker. Nor was it just the ceremonial laws that he seems to have broken, as when he approved of his disciples eating without washing their hands if they had no opportunity to do so (Matt. 15.20; Mark 7.1-9). He seems consistently to have broken the laws attached to the Sabbath (and let us remember that the Fourth Commandment is part of the Decalogue), most usually by healing the sick on the Sabbath day, but on one occasion by permitting his disciples to pluck ears of grain and eat them as they walked through a field of wheat on a Sabbath day (Matt. 12.1 ff.). He seems to have approved of what David did in eating the shewbread (Matt. 12.3; Mark 2.26), an act which must have appeared as sacrilegious to the Pharisees then as a profane eating of the bread or wafer for Holy Communion would strike us today. On the other hand, he was careful to send the leper he had healed to be examined by the priest as the Law prescribed (Matt. 8.4). Is there then inconsistency on Jesus' part in his attitude to the Law? And if there is, then how can he possibly be said to have kept it wholly, and so in any sense to be the *end* of the Law as St Paul declared?

In answering these questions there are two points we must bear in mind: first, the question of the relationship between the written and the oral law; and second, the question of Lord's view of the relationship between the Law of Moses and God's eternal purpose for mankind.

1. *The Oral Law.* We saw in chapter 5 how the word *Torah* had developed to bear two dissimilar interpretations by New Testament times. We saw how the Pharisees had inherited a legalistic view of all that Moses had said and done. Now, this legalistic element within Judaism had learned to stress not only the verbal inerrancy of the Mosaic laws, and to require a punctilious carrying out of their demands in daily life; this element had also by this time begun the process of 'deducing' the laws of the Pentateuch into very many more subsidiary injunctions, thereby designing them to cover all possible eventualities in domestic and public life. The collection of this new material was known as the 'oral law'.

Now, Jesus rejected this 'oral law' altogether. But at the same time he also broke with the frame of mind that felt the need to deduce the Law in this way. He broke with the view that a believing man must regard obedience to God as synonymous with obedience to a multiplicity of regulations. Rabbinical legalism had abandoned the spontaneity of willing obedience which the Psalmists had known and expressed in Old Testament times, when for example one can say in the 119th Psalm: 'O how love I thy *Torah*! it is my meditation all the day' (v. 97). In its place the Rabbis had put in the heart of the ordinary Israelite, not a personal loyalty to God, but a mere anxiety to fulfil the Law's demands. That he had no such anxiety in his own heart is made clear when our Lord failed to observe the Rabbinic prescriptions on such matters as eating with publicans and sinners, as non-obedience to the laws on ritual washings, and in the matter of healing on the Sabbath day.

2. *God's eternal purpose.* This lack of anxiety on his part sprang from two sources. First, Jesus understood the word *Torah*, not as the Rabbis were then expounding it, but in terms of the prophetic interpretation of the Old Testament, one that was as fully his heritage as the other. In this tradition *Torah* is both the record and the revelation of God's saving purpose for the whole world. Within that purpose God's Word through Moses must necessarily play its part. Yet in so far as the Law is second in time to the expression of God's plan of salvation as he makes it known to Abraham, the Law is in reality a servant of the greater whole. Second, Jesus knew himself to be Lord of the *Torah*, in the same sense as he was Lord of the Sabbath. These had been in the beginning with him in the very life of God the Creator (Gen. 2.2-3; John 1.1). Thus Jesus knew that in himself a greater than Moses was here.

In light of the above, let us now examine to see how our Lord dealt with several primary issues as they are embodied in the Law of Moses.

(a) *The Sabbath.* The Sabbath regulations are part of the Law that is both of Moses and yet has been 'deduced' to endless detail by the Rabbis. Under both heads, however, it must subserve God's original purpose of saving love for his world. Yet what do we find happens to the Sabbath in Jesus' day? To suppose that the mighty purposes of God could be focussed on the ridiculous question of *not* eating grains of standing wheat when a man was hungry and was needing food in order to be a 'whole' man, especially when such an action was not regarded as stealing another's property, is to reduce the divine plan to the level of absurdity. On the other hand we see Jesus conscious that he is Lord and not slave of the Law, showing Israel how to be joyfully obedient to the meaning and purpose of the Law even while rejecting the literalistic deductions of the Rabbis. The God of Moses had said: 'I am the Lord that healeth thee,' and he had said so in the very context where he commanded Israel to hearken to his voice and obey all his commandments. This was the perspective, then, that Jesus, the 'Good Physician' indeed, made explicit when he placed a literal obedience to the Law in subservience to God's loving, creative purpose for man. Consequently, in approving the action of his disciples when they ate the grains of wheat, in approving the action of David long before, Christ was declaring that the 'ultimate meaning', the 'end' of the Law, was for the healing, sustaining and saving of men (see also Rom. 3.31; 13.10; Gal. 5.14).

(b) *The Ceremonial Law*. A specific instance of Christ's disregard of the binding nature of the ceremonial law is his attitude to the many lepers who came to him. It is obvious to us that it was a good thing for a leper who had been cured to go and show himself to the priest who was duly appointed to inspect lepers. But it is also obvious that it was not good that any sufferer should have to wait one day longer than is necessary before he could be cured of his racking pain. If the Pharisees, therefore, so interpreted the Law that their interpretation clashed with the conception of the value God placed upon human life in the beginning, then their 'oral law' must be wrong. As Jesus pointed out, this oral law was merely the 'tradition of men' (Mark 7.8), and not the absolute revelation of God's loving will and purpose for the establishment of *shalom* within the life of the Covenant People.

(c) *Marriage and Divorce*. In Mark 10.2 ff. we read: 'The Pharisees came to him, and asked him, Is it lawful for a man to put away his wife? tempting him.' In his reply our

Lord does three things. First, he refers to the Law of Moses,
pointing to the fact that if it came from Moses then it came
from God. Here he clearly differentiates between *Torah* and
the 'oral law'. 'What did Moses command you?' The answer
comes: 'Moses suffered to write a bill of divorcement, and
to put her away.' The allusion is to Deut. 24.1b. Incidentally
we are shown how thoroughly and in what detail both Jesus
and the Pharisees knew their Scriptures. Second, our Lord
judges the Law. This is because he sees it in the light of
God's eternal purpose which he knows has now become flesh
in himself. 'And Jesus answered and said unto them, For
the hardness of your heart he wrote you this precept.' That
is to say, Moses gave Israel legislation on divorce that was
not meant to be an 'absolute'. So long as Israel possessed
only the light that the Law could give, all that could be
expected of human nature was what could be legislated for
in the Law. Jesus does not, however, question the relevance
of the Law as such. What he does do is to comment on it.
In his day the Jewish woman had no rights. According to
the 'liberal' school of Hillel her husband could divorce her
for almost a whim; but the woman could not divorce her
husband unless he became a leper or something equally
disgusting. So what Jesus does is to place the woman on an
equality with the man, in accordance with the principle
expressed in Gen. 2.18 ('I will make him a helper who will
be his equal and opposite number'). Though this story is in
Torah, yet it precedes in time the Law of Moses. Third,
Jesus continues with what lies anterior to the Law of Moses
altogether. He continues to quote: 'But from the beginning
of creation God made them male and female.' That, our
Lord knew, was the divine intention for all humanity, even
before God called Israel to be his people. 'For this cause
shall a man leave his father and mother, and cleave to his
wife; and they twain shall be one flesh: so then they are no

more twain, but one flesh. What therefore God hath joined
together, let not man put asunder.' Thus it is clear that
Jesus believed that the divine intention, as known to and
stated by the authors of Gen. 1 and 2, was summed up and
had now reached its *end* in himself just as the legal precepts
too had found their *end* in him. That this is so becomes
even more evident in our Lord's subsequent discussion of
this topic with his disciples (Mark 10.10-12). In this discussion Jesus once again 'deduced' the Mosaic Law beyond
what was to be found in black and white. In the Law it is
accepted that a man can commit adultery against another
married man; but nowhere that he may possibly commit
adultery against his own wife. This deduction is one that
Jesus alone makes, and it is not to be found in the *Torah*.
Or again, Jesus insists that if a *woman*, this time, divorces
her husband and gets married again, she commits adultery.
This view is not only non-existent in the Moisaic Law, it is
even contrary to it. But, as Jesus declares, such was surely in
accord with God's plan for man and woman in the beginning. The latter, then, the reference to Gen. 2.24, is *Torah*
in its greater fulness rather than the precept to be found in
Deut. 24.1b. By making this important point, to do which
he had to go *behind* the legal element in *Torah*, our Lord
linked the original purpose of God for men and women with
that purpose now made explicit in his own teaching and
mission in his attitude to women. He thereby gives marriage a position of the highest dignity, clearly regarding it
as an indissoluble union; and at the same time he places
husband and wife in a relationship of equality such as had
never been known before in the world's history. The particular fascinating fact of which we need to be aware for our
purposes, however, is that Jesus' attitude to women, which
is such an attractive feature of the Gospels, and which we
are inclined to regard as 'new' in the sense of the previous

sentence, Jesus himself regarded not as new at all. What he was declaring in the discussions we have recorded in Mark 10 was that such a view of women and of marriage was in fact God's original plan, that it is in fact to be found recorded in *Torah*, despite a toning down of its high demands to meet a temporary situation, and that that plan has found its *end* now in Christ himself and in what he was there and then doing for women and for marriage in the purpose of God that had become incarnate in himself.

Again, the succeeding conversation on riches (Mark 10.23 ff.) must have sounded strange to Jewish ears. This is because the Law of Moses gives us no hint at all that wealth could be a barrier to entering into the kingdom of God. But further examples need not be cited.

We have established this point that our Lord regarded himself as the embodiment of God's original purpose for mankind. That purpose was later expressed in an imperfect manner in the Law of Moses. As such, generations of the People of God had accepted it and sought to put it into practice, and so had sought to bring into being the *shalom* of which it spoke. 'The Law was given by Moses,' indeed. But in aeons long before Moses' day grace and truth had been present with the Father in the person of the Son. That is why St Paul can say: 'Our fathers . . . were all baptized unto Moses in the cloud and in the sea . . . they drank of that spiritual Rock that followed them: and that Rock was Christ' (I Cor. 10.1-4). The *end* of the Law of Moses was therefore also grace and truth. Thus every jot and tittle of the Law of Moses had found its ultimate significance in the eternal Word made flesh in the form of Jesus of Nazareth.

A most interesting outcome of the argument outlined above is now clearly seen as follows. The 'wholeness' of the Christian faith is to be found only when the witness of the two Testaments is allowed to play upon each other, and when it is grasped that the Gospel must rest upon Law, and Law must be fulfilled in Gospel. This is true even though the Law has only a temporary significance in the purposes of God. The Word of God must stand for ever (Isa. 40.8; I Peter 1.25), on the ground that God is faithful to himself. Thus the Law of Moses, being no less than the Word of God himself, is not annulled in Christ, but fulfilled, and takes on a new lease of life, so to speak, at a higher level of being.

It has been suggested that Micah 6.8 contains a summary of Old Testament religion: 'What does the Lord require of you, O mankind, but to bring about a condition of real social justice, to be utterly loyal to God's covenant love, and to have a vital personal faith in God himself?' This is the picture of a society that is living in the spirit of that *shalom* of which the Law of Moses gives us the 'rules'. But this ideal is unattainable for Old Testament man, and remains to mock him in all his efforts; for it reminds him that as a sinner he is under judgment for not attaining to this ideal. But in Christ, on the other hand, this ideal of Micah's faith is finally met. Jesus said: '*Shalom* I leave with you, my *shalom* I give unto you; not as the world giveth, give I unto you' (John 14.27). And so the great heritage of Israel now becomes a greater heritage still.

Yet Jesus provides us with the key to open the door into this new heritage from out of the Law of Moses! He takes one passage from Deuteronomy and another from Leviticus and places them together as one: 'The first of all the commandments is, Hear, O Israel; the Lord our God is one Lord: and thou shalt love the Lord thy God with all thy heart, and with all thy soul, and with all thy mind, and with all thy strength: this is the first commandment. And the second is like, namely this, Thou shalt love thy neighbour as thyself' (Mark 12.29-31; Deut. 6.4-5; Lev. 19.18; and cf.

Gal. 3.6-9). It is at this point, then, that Jesus' phrase '. . . but I say unto you' takes on new clarity and relevance.

Dr Karl Barth has written of the significance of time with a clarity we can do well to envy. 'Without time', he writes,[1] 'it would be impossible to have a promise, and without a promise it would be unbearable to have time. Christ's coming into the world fulfils both the promise and time.' ' "The promise is fulfilled" does not mean it has ceased and what is promised takes its place. It means . . . what is promised is complete, and thus *potent*.' This analogy of Christ's fulfilment of 'time' that Dr Karl Barth makes surely helps us to see how Christ fulfils the Law as well, not thereby destroying the Law and setting it aside now as irrelevant, but rather making it *potent*. The Law now takes on, indeed, a *new* significance owing to the great significance of him who is its *end*. This conception we might illustrate from still another biblical motif, that of the analogy of the Temple that our Lord himself used, and which we have raised before: 'This fellow said, I am able to destroy the temple of God, and to build it in three days' (Matt. 26.61). 'Destroy this temple and in three days I will raise it up' (John 2.19). It is quite clear to us, as we now look back upon the whole sweep of events recorded in both the Testaments, how Christ can be regarded as the new *form* of the ancient Temple. Through the sacrifices of the old Temple men found reconciliation with God. Reconciliation has not now ended, however, now that Jerusalem has been destroyed, and now that Christ has 'fulfilled' the purpose of the Temple! Far from it. Reconciliation with God has now taken on a new depth and power such as the old Temple had never been able to offer. What had happened was that the old Temple had merely met its *end* in Christ. In the same way, then, the Law has not just been 'ended' by

[1] *Christmas*, trans. B. Citron, 1959, pp. 35, 39.

Christ. He himself is its *end*. That then is why the Law cannot simply be discarded as clothes are discarded that have now been worn out and should be thrown away.

Up till now we have emphasized that the revelation given us in Christ is 'new' in the sense that it 'fills full' the old. We have seen that the Greeks described that kind of newness by the adjective *kainos*. But we indicated earlier that there is another word for 'new' as well, viz. *neos*. There is no doubt that Jesus is as truly this kind of 'new' as he is the other. The New Testament places him in the very centre of all life, all revelation, and all God's redemptive purpose, and it does so in such a manner as to regard him as not merely the fulfilment of the old, but actually also as something shockingly new (I Cor. 1.23). In light of this then, and because Jesus himself declared '. . . but I say unto you', the Church has learned to interpret and obey the *Torah* in the light of Christ, and not Christ in the light of *Torah*. Jesus and his work are in fact not only the *end* of *Torah*, they are also unique in their efficacy. One phrase for this uniqueness of the work of Christ is that it is 'once-for-all' (Rom. 6.10; Heb. 7.27). The Fourth Gospel expresses this uniqueness of Christ very simply: he is 'from above' (John 8.23). Since this is so, then Jesus must have set the stamp of his own uniqueness upon the Law that was finding its *end* in him.

We read in Matt. 5.21-22 that Jesus quoted the Sixth Commandment with approval. But now in his 'new' teaching, and in his new life, the commandment 'Thou shalt not kill' becomes more than a mere command written on a statute book. It now becomes a command written on the heart, to use Jeremiah's phrase of old. In Jesus this item of the total Word had now become flesh, and so had met its *end* at last. As a child, Jesus had certainly learned the Decalogue at his mother's knee. As an adolescent, he may have discussed its all-embracing significance with the doctors of the law. Probably he had listened to their arguments on issues related to the command 'Thou shalt not kill' such as (to use our modern terms) the problem of euthanasia, the problem of the genocide of a race, the problem of pacifism, the problem of suicide in a righteous cause, and so on. But now, for the first time in history, the Sixth Commandment was no longer a commandment exterior to the man for whom it was intended, a commandment merely to be discussed, understood and followed. It had now become the man himself. This fact we can set forth in a few sentences. The wages of sin is death. The whole race of mankind has been under the judgment of the just and righteous God, because all men at all times have been sinners. But in willingly accepting his own death in the place of sinful man Jesus 'saved' mankind from earning the wages it should have received; and so he healed men of all their diseases, even the final disease of death. By dying, Jesus abolished death (2 Tim. 1.10). Knowing, moreover, what he had come into the world to do, it is understandable that the Good Physician, in that freedom which is to be expected of the Master of the Commandment, should enlarge the scope and depth of the Sixth Commandment to the ultimate degree that it can attain. Now it has to reach down to the depths of the unspeakably evil imaginations of men's hearts, as well as answer the intolerable wickedness with which men handle each other, whether by crucifixion in days of old, or by the H-bomb in our own time. And it has to reach even beyond what we call physical death into that area of God's rule or kingdom which we call the life to come, that area to which we have referred when we spoke of the 'meaningfulness' of men's actions upon this earth. It has to reach even to where the ultimate significance of men's rejection of God's sacrificial love for them *here and now* becomes apparent *there and then*—it has to reach down even to hell: 'But I say unto you, that everyone who is angry with his brother shall be liable to judgment; whosoever insults his brother shall be liable to the council, and whosoever says, "You fool", shall be liable to the hell of fire' (Matt. 5.22 RSV). Such an ultimate deduction from the Sixth Commandment follows in a direction totally opposite to that observable in the oral law of the Pharisees. It is made to meet, not the symptoms of disease, but the disease itself that attacks a man in the depths of his soul. It is not in any sense the abrogation of the Law. Rather it is quite literally the 'fill-fulment' of the Law, and in a manner that would have been impossible even for our Lord if he had not begun by accepting Ex. 20.13 as basically the Word of God. 'For verily I say unto you, Till heaven and earth pass, one jot or one tittle shall in no wise pass from the law, till all be fulfilled' (Matt. 5.18).

Thus our Lord is *kainos*; he is the *end* of the Law, and 'new' in the sense that he fulfils the Word of God as made known through Moses. But he is also *neos*; he is that new, unique, divine event without precedent in the history of the world. In Christ, those two aspects of the word 'new' are united. He is both the *end* of the Law and the action of God for the salvation of both earth and heaven. In himself he unites both earth and heaven, both the Law of Moses and God's eternal purpose for all worlds. So we can say of him, not only 'was crucified, dead and buried', but also 'he descended into hell'. Yet since this same Jesus has also ascended to the right hand of God, he has therefore taken up in himself into the realm of 'ultimate significance' the ancient Law of Moses which had become flesh in him when he dwelt in Palestine. The Law of Moses is therefore now no longer the 'law of commandments' (Eph. 2.15). In Christ it is now become the law of the life of the Spirit.

13

The Christian and the Law of Moses

IT is now time for us to offer a resolute answer to the question whether a Christian should keep the Law of Moses. Yet the answer, as the reader will now be aware, can be given only in terms of both 'yes' and 'no'. 'No', if the Christian supposes that by keeping the Law, he is saved thereby. 'No', if he supposes that a literal obedience to the Law is required of him as the Pharisees required it of the Jews in New Testament times. But 'yes', if he can see that when he commits himself to Christ, he is putting himself in total obedience under him who is the *end* of the Law in the sense that we have examined.

In the first place, then, the Christian is not saved by the keeping of the Law. No man can earn salvation by doing what the Law prescribes. Paul is adamant on that point. 'A man is not justified by the works of the Law . . . for by the works of the Law shall no flesh be justified; but by the faith of Jesus Christ . . . that we might be justified by the faith of Christ, and not by the works of the Law' (Gal. 2.16). 'Ye are not under the Law, but under Grace' (Rom. 6.14). 'This only would I learn of you, Received ye the Spirit by the works of the law, or by the hearing of faith?' (Gal. 3.2). In the light of these clear statements, it is obvious that if a man tries to live in perfection by keeping the Law of Moses wholly and completely, then one of two things will happen to him. Either he will lose heart, because no man can perfectly keep the Law, or else he will become a Pharisee (in the popular sense of that term). That is to say, he will learn to pride himself upon his own attainment in being able to keep the Law. Such pride is obviated for those who rest in confidence in what Christ has done for them already, and who believe utterly that their salvation stems from the work of Christ alone. What they therefore know within their hearts is not pride, but joy and gratitude.

Yet even at this point the Law is of undoubted value, says St Paul in Rom. 7.7 ff. In the course of the important and profound argument in this chapter, Paul declares that we would not in fact realize how truly we are sinners if the Law had not first declared to us 'Thou shalt not covet'. The Law would not have needed to speak in this way at all if men such as we had never known what it was to covet. But if it had not spoken as it did, then we would not have felt the need for a Saviour to save us from our sins. The Law has thus done us a very important service. Then Paul projects the origin of the Law to a period even before the time of Moses and the giving of the Law on Sinai. He postulates its existence even in the Garden of Eden. His argument is based on the fact that Adam himself came to know the reality of Law at the moment when the fruit of the tree was forbidden him. For this reason, says Paul, the Law itself is a holy thing; in serving Adam (and us) it shows itself to be just, so that God established it for our good. It is a necessary instrument of the Holy God as he seeks to reveal himself to man.

We are to be careful to recognize, St Paul continues, that the Law is under no circumstances to be confused with sin. Sin came on the scene only at the moment when Adam (and we!) had made use for own self-centred ends of this good thing that God had given us. What the Law has actually done for us then is to show up sin to be what it really is in itself. Sin is not the Law, therefore it is not the

Law that we are to blame when we fall into sin; it is the
weakness of our will that is at fault. In fact 'I cordially
agree with God's Law' Paul declares at the conclusion of his
argument (Rom. 7.22 Moffatt), for the Law is essentially
God's instrument to bring man to a knowledge of his need
of salvation.

But there is the contrary point of view as well. It is a mis-
taken understanding of the thought of Paul, and of Martin
Luther too, for that matter, to suppose that for both those
great exponents of the Christian Faith all that is asked of
man is to have faith in Christ. This is because both are
fully aware that the New Testament clearly presents man
with a challenge to keep 'law' just as surely as it summons
him to accept the Gospel. This antinomy we must now
examine.

After all that has been said above, it is important to note
what a central place moral instruction takes in the New
Testament. In his Epistles Paul insouciantly steps from
profound theological discussion to demanding of his
readers and hearers obedience to a very practical code of
ethics. We notice, for example, that immediately following
upon the exacting analysis of the relationship between pre-
destination and freewill that comprises the contents of Rom.
9-11, in chapters 12 and 13 he turns to deal with everyday
and commonplace morality: 'Distributing to the necessity
of saints; given to hospitality' (12.13); 'Render therefore to
all their dues: tribute to whom tribute is due . . . owe no
man anything' (13.7-8). Thereupon, in Rom. 13.9-10, Paul
makes reference to Christ's summary of the Ten Commandments given us in the so-called 'Law of Love'. In v. 7 of the
same chapter Paul quotes Christ's saying, 'Render unto
Caesar the things that are Caesar's, and unto God the things
that are God's.' Thus in quoting Christ, he is giving moral
instruction, and he does so on the ground that he believes

that Christ has done it before him. Paul's converts had come out of the, morally speaking, very lax society of the Roman Empire. Both to the Corinthians and to the Thessalonians therefore he finds that he must give guiding rules of conduct on sexual matters. These rules he even calls his own 'commandments' (I Cor. 7.25; I Thess. 4.2). The Epistle to the Hebrews, I Peter, and the Pastoral Epistles, all reflect the same peremptory tone on moral issues above (see Heb. 13.1-3; I Peter 2.11-18).

On the other hand, we read that St Paul objected to his converts keeping the Sabbath and the Old Testament festivals in the Jewish way in a literal sense (Gal. 4.10). He disagreed with them also when they were unwilling to eat meat that was unclean in the Levitical sense of the word (I Cor. 8). The reason for his objection is now clear to us. The *literal* observance of the command to keep the Sabbath, for example, can only stifle the explosive power latent within the command itself. The early Church was therefore acting in full conformity with the mind of Christ who had become in himself the *end* of the Fourth Commandment, when it allowed Sabbath observance to burst out of the bondage of the Law into the joyous freedom of those who observe a day that has now been orientated elsewhere. Since the outcome of the Mosaic Law was clearly seen to be the ethics of the Kingdom of Heaven, or, to use modern theological jargon again, since the early Church recognized that the eschatological significance of the Mosaic Law had now been revealed in the risen Christ, the Sabbath day had found its *end* in him. The observance of the Lord's Day was, of course, still rooted in the Law of Moses. It was still every seventh day that was observed, and observed as a rest from all that hindered man from worshipping God. But now it was regarded as the first-fruits of the Sabbath rest of heaven, available to the Church on earth, on the ground that heaven is no less than the ultimate eschatological expression of the *shalom* that Christ has brought into the world in fulfilment of the 'peace' that God promised to Israel through the Law of Moses.

But, as we have said, our Lord himself seems to have laid down laws for moral behaviour when he said, 'But I say unto you . . .' In fact, in I Cor. 13 Paul presents us with a vignette of a man who is now living by those laws of Christ. So far from feeling embarrassed by the idea that Christ has given us law, we ought therefore to accept his guidance with satisfaction.

We concluded the previous chapter by declaring that the New Testament Epistles regard the Law in two lights at once, first as a temporary institution given to Israel for her good for a period only, and second, as a revelation that finds its fulfilment in Christ, now enjoying a new potency that it never possessed before. The two points are made clear also in our Lord's own utterances, when he handles the question of the Mosaic Law.

The Sermon on the Mount has been called 'the New Law' by some who have noticed the parallel between the giving of the Law on Mount Sinai and Christ's 'opening his mouth' and teaching the 'Word' on the mount of the Beatitudes. There is indeed a parallel. The Law of Moses was meant to be legislation for the People of God as they sought the good life within the Covenant relationship that God had imposed upon them. In the same way the Sermon on the Mount may be said to contain the Law of the Kingdom of Christ. But this new law reveals a new way of life, one that is attainable only by those who are truly 'in Christ', and who therefore are indeed 'blessed'. It is an ideal, however, that the Sermon on the Mount expresses, for individuals and for the Church alike, towards which both must ever strive so long as they live upon this earth. Both must recognize that the attainment of the ideal is always out of reach, because this new 'Law' is the revelation (*Torah*) of the bonds that unite those who are already passed into heaven.

'The Law of Christ works by setting up a process within us which is itself ethical activity. Christ's precepts stir the imagination, arouse the conscience, challenge thought, and give an impetus to the will, issuing in action. In so far as we respond . . . there gradually comes to be built up in us a certain outlook on life, a bias of mind, a standard of moral judgment.'[1]

We are now in the position where we can see clearly the direct line of relation between the Law of Moses and the Law of Christ. We have realized that the Law of Moses is temporary, and that before it was given on Mount Sinai God's promises looked forward to what would come even after its function was complete. But the Law of Moses was temporary only in that it has found its *end* in Christ. This 'end', not being the end of a series, does not mean that the Law of Moses is now past and forgotten. In Christ it has found a new potency and validity, and has taken on a wholly new dimension, so profoundly new that those who love the old may even hate it for its newness. The weakness of the Old Covenant with its Law lay not in the Law itself. It lay in the weakness of Israel's faith. The New Covenant, on the other hand, is strong, because of the faith, not of man, but of Christ (Gal. 3.16). The perfect faith of Christ may thus still express itself in terms of law—the Law of Christ. The Law of Love now subsumes the Law of Moses, and reinterprets it so that the latter can be applied in principle to any and every situation in any century of the world's history. The verb *pleroun*, which is used of 'fulfilling', means something like the releasing of the poten-

[1] C. H. Dodd, *Gospel and Law*, 1951, p. 77.

tial in the Law of Moses so that it becomes, not just word, but action. This action is now operative in wholly new ways, though we can see that the action is still rooted in the Law of Moses. It is no longer the expression of the ethical teaching which the ancient world was full of. Palestine in Jesus' day had its choice of the ethical systems of the Stoics and the Epicureans, and of the moral advice of many poets and philosophers speaking and writing in many languages. Nor is it any longer identical with the ethical teaching of the Jewish communities that covered the whole Mediterranean world, even though the Jews were the cleanest living and the most moral people that the world had ever seen. No, the Law of Christ represents a profoundly new situation that has arisen once the commands of the old Law are allowed to burst their bonds, like wine bursting out of the wine-skin that held it. The potency of the divine Word, first addressed to Moses, and through him to Israel, and now finding its *end* in Christ, becomes an explosive force that produces effects that man does not bring about by merely being obedient to legal precepts. Instead of giving an eye for an eye, the new man in Christ now finds himself turning his other cheek. Instead of sueing another at the law because he has stolen his coat, the new man in Christ finds himself giving the culprit his cloak also. Instead of walking one mile to show a man the way, the new man in Christ finds himself going not one but two. Instead of forgiving once, he finds himself forgiving seventy times seven. 'What do ye more (than the Law prescribes)?' we understand Christ to ask (Matt. 5.47).

Since the wonderful new dimension in life that Christ offers us seems to remove us far from the spirit of mere legalism, then what connection does obedience to this new Law of Love have to the old Law of Moses? 'Much every way,' as Paul might have answered. Indeed, in answering the original question that we have had in mind from the beginning, we should declare explicitly that the Christian who seeks to live close to his Lord in the modern world is keeping the Law of Moses essentially, even though he is unconscious of the fact. There is thus a very intimate connection between leading the Christian life and keeping the ancient Law. The reality of this connection may be observed in the faith both of individuals and in the strivings of the Church to create a better society.

First, the individual believer. Christ may quote a precept from the *Torah*, thereby acknowledging it to be part of the Word of God, not a jot or tittle of which shall pass 'till all be fulfilled', and then do something with that 'word' which is wholly new. He who is the *end* of the Law himself now empowers it to unfold its true meaning and produce its predestined effect in a new fulness of vitality in the life of the man who is joined with him. But when he does this with the precept in question, Christ does not thereupon offer the believer a new law or a new precept that he himself is inventing on the spot. He is offering him an ancient precept from the Law of Moses. And this is true even of the so-called 'Eleventh Commandment' which we are inclined to attribute to Christ alone, but which our Lord is merely quoting out of Deuteronomy and Leviticus. This means that it is in fact the Law of Moses which is the original Word of God, but that it is Christ, the living Word, who is the agency that releases the potentiality within it. There is nowhere any suggestion that the wisdom of the Stoics could thus find a release and a new power in the way that does in fact happen with the Law of Moses. Going the second mile, forgiving a man seventy times seven, turning the other cheek—all these commands with their new content and exciting possibilities issue in the first place from the W of God which cannot return unto him void. Their all to be found in the *Torah* which God gave to his people through the hand of Moses.

Second, social justice. The Law of Moses reveals God's insistent requirement here. The *Torah*, when applied to human society, was meant to produce a brotherhood under God such as could offer Israel a blue-print for a truly peaceful co-existence. Jewry has always possessed a magnificent sense of solidarity, whenever its members have been loyal to the precepts of the *Torah*. A Jew in Buenos Aires in the 1960s will recognize his oneness with a Jew in Denmark or Australia in a manner that transcends the barriers of politics or even war. In days of terror and flight Jews contributed unquestionably more for the relief of Jews in trouble than the Church did for Christians who similarly sought its aid. Small, not very wealthy, Jewish communities in many parts of the world welcomed as brethren total strangers from the ends of the earth, and at once pooled their resources to set those newcomers on their feet again. Christendom has not yet attained to this great solidarity, for loyalty to one's nation still means more than loyalty to one's brethren in Christ in other lands. This is because Christians have not yet rightly appreciated where their roots do in fact lie, nor allowed themselves to be properly 'grafted into Israel' whose way of life was patterned long ago in the Law of Moses. The Mosaic pattern of life is therefore not an alternative to the Gospel; it is part of the Gospel.

The Christian ought to feel himself bound closer to his brother Christian in a foreign country than to his unbelieving next-door neighbour. This is because the 'morality' which the early Church taught is not a morality that is attainable by a man's own efforts and that is independent ith. It is the morality that is specially revealed to the People, a morality attainable only within the bonds of the Covenant. But since the Mosaic Covenant has now met its end and fulfilment in Christ, then to live within the Covenant—or in our case, to be a member of the Christian Church—means to live in the atmosphere of a new morality not to be found outside the walls of the Church. This is still the morality of the Old Covenant; but that Covenant is now extended to comprehend the fellowship of all the redeemed, a fellowship that transcends all national and political barriers. The rediscovery of 'Law' as part of the Gospel is consequently more essential in our day than ever before. By its recovery alone can the Church present the world with that wholeness and fulness of its faith which it is meant to preach and practise.

When the modern Christian builds a house, he still needs to be reminded to put a balustrade round the roof, so that his friends shall not fall off (Deut. 22.8), even though the essence of that command may now have to be translated into very different terms within the complexities of modern life. He must still lead back a strayed ox or ass to its rightful owner (Deut. 22.1-3), even though the command has to be understood in terms of motor-cars and lawn-mowers. Very obviously he must still ensure in ways that the ancient world could never have envisaged that he does not have in his 'bag divers weights, a great and a small . . . but a perfect and just weight' (Deut. 25.13-16). Exciting new horizons have opened up for him that go far beyond the literal fulfilment of the Law even when the Law is adapted to modern life. The explosive power of the Word now carries him forward to work out new experiments in human relations. He sees that he is called to put the Law (of Moses, fulfilled in Christ) into effective, vital, living activity. In doing so, he is paradoxically no longer obedient to Law at all; rather he freely expressing his unbounded gratitude and love to Christ for what Christ has done for him.

Finally, the vital continuity of the Law of Moses with the new Law of Christ is made plain when we recall what we said earlier about the 'eschatological significance' of the Law of Moses. In the Sermon on the Mount we are allowed to glimpse the reality of those two technical theological terms, for that 'Sermon' contains the ethics, not of earth, but of the Kingdom of God. Here even the sacrificial laws find their end and meaning. In Ps. 50.7 the believing servant of God shows an awareness, even in the Old Testament period, that the Mosaic laws on sacrifice were of a temporary nature. But now the sacrifice on the Cross has wholly re-orientated the intrinsic nature and content of those laws on sacrifice. When the early Christians gave up participating in the Temple sacrifices they were not in effect giving up loyalty to the Law of Moses; for the new man in Christ discovers that if he presents his *own* body as a living sacrifice it will be no less than his reasonable service (Rom. 12.1), and his due response to Christ's supreme sacrifice on the Cross of Calvary.

The Christian who has been redeemed by the Cross of Christ, and who responds to what God has done for him in Christ by taking up his own cross daily and following him, is all unwittingly therefore sharing in the *end* of the Law of Moses as the latter has been transformed in Christ. In doing so, then, the Christian is living according to a Law which, having had its source in God in the beginning, and which God later mediated to Israel by Moses, was finally set free from its legal bonds by Christ to burst forth out of its old wine-skins and become the Law of the life of the Kingdom. We may thus even go so far as to say that the ancient Law of Moses, as part of the *Torah* that is synonymous with first five books of the Old Testament, is the very foun-
framework of the life of the redeemed of God in the
hat is above and that is to come.

EPILOGUE

Jews and Christians

JEWS and Christians are thus linked intimately together. Both are rooted in the Law of Moses. Yet how tragic their contacts and relationships have been since biblical days. In AD 70 the Romans razed Jerusalem to the ground. Jews were no longer permitted even to live in the Holy Land. Since then their history has been one of persecution and flight, caused largely by those who have espoused the name of Christ. In our generation the Jews have met two transforming experiences. One has been the Hitlerian massacres, and the other, partly a consequence of the first, has been the constitution, in 1948, of the new state of Israel.

This word 'Israel', however, has several connotations, and these we should be interested to tabulate. (1) Israel was the name used in the Old Testament for the Northern Kingdom that the Assyrians took into exile in 721 BC. (2) Israel was the name in the Old Testament also of all the sons of the patriarch Jacob, who was later known as Israel. Consequently the sons of Israel, or simply 'Israel' as one collective entity, became the name borne by the whole Covenant People of God. When this people came out of Egypt, however, they comprised not merely the blood-related sons of Jacob, but also a 'mixed multitude' of many racial origins. (3) Israel is the name chosen by the returning Jews for that part of the Holy Land where, since 1948, they have been able to establish their new and flourishing national home and state. (4) Israel is the name for the People of God as a

whole into which the Christian believer is grafted when he
is baptised in the name of Israel's God. And so 'Israel' can
cover the whole Christian Church throughout the world
today, a 'mixed multitude' indeed. A local congregation
thus finds itself repeating the words about itself: 'If it had
not been the Lord who was on our side, now may Israel
say . . .' (Ps. 124). This is because the local church is as
much the heritor of the Psalmist's words as are the members of the local synagogue. On the other hand our Jewish
friends will insist, and rightly, that not only they are 'Israel',
their land too is 'Israel', and that because it has been so for
three thousand years.

We who are Christians are therefore bound up with the
Jews by a word. May it be that a new appreciation of that
word in our day can build a bridge to end the centuries of
calumny and shame between us? For we are to remember
that the word 'Israel' has no plural. This fact requires us to
recognise that there can only be one Israel. Accordingly,
the Church cannot be regarded as the 'new Israel' and seek
to displace the Jews on the ground that they are just the
'old Israel'. Neither the idea of this nor the word 'new' in
connection with the word 'Israel' occurs anywhere in the
New Testament. This is because, as we said, there is but
one Israel of God, and one Covenant; there is just the
'ancient' covenant that is later renewed in Christ. In that
one Israel, therefore, Jews and Christians must necessarily
share. It was the one Israel that was called to be the Servant
of God (Isa. 42.1-6). 'Every city or house divided against
itself shall not stand', Jesus once warned his People Israel
(Matt. 12.25). In the service of God together, therefore, Jews
and Christians must not only reverse the vicious trend of
the past two millenia, they must rediscover their common
brotherhood; and within the bond of that brotherhood together seek to study and then to obey the Word of God.

Now, no Christian can say that the Church has whole-heartedly appropriated and put into practice in the economic and social life of man that *shalom* which Moses spoke of in the 'Law'. Nor can any Jew declare that he has experienced the compulsion and hilarious joy of being born again in Christ, so that he knows what it is to possess power sufficient to break down the barriers that create confusion and discord. As Ben Chorin has said of Paul's rebirth on the Damascus Road: 'We Jews have not been down that road.' But that road of Grace Moses understood even in days of 'Law'. Perhaps the day may come, then, once the chasm between Jew and Christian is even partly bridged, when the Christian will discover virtually for the first time in history what the *shalom* of the Torah can mean for the social life of man; and the Jew will discover, but only within the setting of 'the adoption, and the glory, and the covenants, and the giving of the law, and the service of God, and the promises', certainly not outside of all these things, what it means to be born again in Christ. For the 'glory' that had appeared at Sinai rested upon Christ at his Transfiguration. There it was that 'Moses', the living executor of the Law, along with 'Elijah', the prophetic interpreter of the Law, witnessed as one to him who is both the fill-fullment, as well as the catalyst, of the Law. They witnessed to the reality that the Law of Moses is more 'alive' in Christ than Moses could ever have supposed his Law could be, and that it has in fact become the Law of the Kingdom of heaven.

The Church has therefore an abiding and imperative commission to proclaim Christ to that other portion of the Covenant People of God who have not yet understood that it is Christ who interprets to them their existence as Israel, and who fulfils in himself the meaning of their existence and calling. Yet, since the Church has still so much to learn from these its brethren who dwell together with it within the bonds of the one Covenant about the meaning of the redemption of the whole social order and communal life of man, both Church and Synagogue must humbly listen to what the other has to say to its 'siamese twin'. Not only has each much to teach the other, each has much to learn from the other; and so the confrontation of Church and Synagogue must go forward, and go forward it must, only in the form of warm-hearted and humble dialogue, as each informs the other of the wonders of God's love.

INDEX OF BIBLICAL REFERENCES

INDEX OF SUBJECTS